The Romance of English Almshouses

Also from Westphalia Press
westphaliapress.org

The Romance of English Almshouses

by Mary F. Raphael

WESTPHALIA PRESS
An Imprint of Policy Studies Organization

Westphalia Press
An imprint of Policy Studies Organization
1527 New Hampshire Ave., NW
Washington, D.C. 20036
info@ipsonet.org

ISBN-13: 978-1-63391-621-0
ISBN-10: 1-63391-621-9

Cover design by Jeffrey Barnes:
jbarnesbook.design

Daniel Gutierrez-Sandoval, Executive Director
PSO and Westphalia Press

Updated material and comments on this edition
can be found at the Westphalia Press website:
www.westphaliapress.org

THE ROMANCE OF ENGLISH
ALMSHOUSES

The Almshouses, St. Cross
Winchester

THE ROMANCE OF
ENGLISH ALMSHOUSES

BY

MARY F. RAPHAEL

AUTHOR OF "THE LURE OF THE LOIRE"

WITH 26 ILLUSTRATIONS FROM PHOTOGRAPHS AND
21 LINE DRAWINGS BY THE AUTHOR

MILLS & BOON, LIMITED
49 RUPERT STREET
LONDON, W. 1

CONTENTS

ILLUSTRATIONS

PHOTOGRAPHS

7

DRAWINGS

FOREWORD

IT was recently my good fortune, during a spacious spring holiday, to pass leisurely through the highways of Dorset. Overhead, swelling clouds raced across a rain-washed faint blue sky. On either side bare purple hedgerows were just beginning to show the promise of tender leaves. From the hazel branches young catkins swung in the breeze.

This new gay air that Nature wore was infectious. I felt exhilarated, as if I were on the verge of some delightful discovery. And presently, as I rounded a corner, I caught sight of a quaint old building set serenely in its little garden. On inquiry I found that it was an ancient almshouse, and I was invited to step in.

From this haphazard visit sprang the wish inspiring a wider quest. For the whole place so charmed and interested me that I was moved to devote my holiday, and sundry future ones—the Fates finding out a way—to search for other dwellings of the kind in various parts of the country.

As a first step I consulted all the books I could discover that dealt with this attractive subject. Not many are to be had, but those I was lucky enough to meet with are rich in information. After studying them, I set forth in hopeful mood on my travels.

I found, however, that to write of all the old almshouses in England would fill a far bulkier volume than the present, and would certainly weary even the well-disposed reader, for in our own country in mediæval times there were, it seems, nearly eight hundred such institutions. But some at least of the outstanding houses are here considered, and several less notable are touched upon, because I found them irresistible.

I was indeed often embarrassed by the abundance of my subject-matter. Selection, with so large a choice at hand, grew difficult, so that a longing to be widely inclusive had to be sternly repressed.

Very reluctantly, therefore, I have been obliged to devote no more than small paragraphs to many attractive and interesting houses of alms, such as St Bartholomew's (Newbury), Hall's (Bradford-on-Avon), Williamson's (Stamford), the Livery Dole (Exeter), and others. And those at Sandwich, Totnes, Moretonhampstead, Stratford-on-Avon, and Clun I am only able to name here, while to wander as far afield as our northern English counties has been impossible.

Within the area to which time and the scope of this volume limited me, however, the work has proved a true labour of love, and so I venture to hope that some of the pleasure its framing has given me may have crept into these pages.

I must record my indebtedness to Mr Sidney Heath's study of *Old English Houses of Alms*, with its interesting drawings, to Miss Rotha M. Clay's *English Mediæval Hospitals*, to Dollman's *Ancient Domestic Architecture*, to Hutchins' *History of Dorset*, as well as to Leland, to Dugdale, and to various other authorities, guide-books, etc.

My thanks are also due to the Lady Warden of the Hungerford Almshouses, Corsham, to the Rev. E. Owen, Higham Ferrers, to the Rev. L. S. Lewis, Glastonbury, to Captain and Mrs Godley at Bruton, to Philip Palmer, Esq., Guildford, to the Rev. Canon Standen, Stamford, to H. J. Carpenter, Esq., Tiverton, and to many others who have assisted me.

Finally, I must add that for all the kindness and courtesy which have been shown to me everywhere, and that have greatly helped me in my search, I cannot be sufficiently grateful.

MARY F. RAPHAEL.

LONDON,
May 1926.

THE ROMANCE OF
ENGLISH ALMSHOUSES

THE HOSPITAL OF ST CROSS, WINCHESTER

TUCKED away in a most attractive corner of Hampshire is the city of Winchester, and the charming
ancient place is further graced by its picturesque
and old-world suburb, formerly called Sparkford,
which contains the greatly renowned almshouse of
St Cross. I therefore set out one happy morning of
early spring to make its acquaintance.

My route skirted the waters of Southampton West,
and on this rare day of grey and gold and shining
blue, wide stretches of marshy land and water glittered in the sun, while the countless green islets of
that sedgy soil provided harbourage for innumerable
seagulls. They crowded together between the glistening pools of water on those bright patches of
emerald, and seemed to have borrowed their whiteness
from the dazzling clouds above, and to have fluttered
down like giant snowflakes from the gleaming sky
itself.

At Winchester, firmly resisting the temptation to
dally within the Cathedral, I sped along a straight ⟍
road that became more rural every few yards.

Little stone cottages with thatched roofs, and others of rough massive stone, defied the passage of time. Their sturdy solidity rejoiced me. What a significant challenge it offers to the quick-building methods of to-day ! A turning to the left near a timbered buff-washed house soon led to the entrance gate of the Hospital.

I applied at the master's house, and a smiling maid readily gave permission from him to use my camera within the precincts. Walking through the outer courtyard, with its old brewhouse dated early in the seventeenth century, I reached the Beaufort Tower. Here, from the porter's hatchway, is still distributed every day a dole of light tawny beer and many slices of bread. This dole is granted to all applicants until the daily rations are exhausted. Scantier portions, be it said, fall to the share of the more affluent and therefore less hungry visitors.

Passing under the Beaufort Tower, the first sight of the wide grassy quadrangle beyond fills one with surprise and pleasure. In the centre of the spacious square stands a white stone sundial. The quadrangle is enclosed on the left by a long ambulatory that adjoins the old Church of St Cross, lying at the south. To the right are the almshouses, a wonderful row of serene little buildings, each adorned with a high chimney. Yes, adorned, for these soaring stacks rise from buttresses implanted in the ground, and add a feature, fascinating and original, giving to the dwellings a charming personal touch, as it

were, of their own. On the north side is the Hundred
Men's Hall—a most entrancing place, with which we
will deal later. It forms the connecting link between
the Beaufort Tower and the last of the almshouses.

Roughly I have here named the principal buildings
of St Cross; but the Hospital has a characteristic distinction peculiar to itself—an individual aura, as it
were, and it is impossible to reproduce in words the
simplicity and peace of the ancient spot. Standing
there, one is transported back into past centuries,
so that the brothers, in their quaint old gowns and
their beef-eater hats, whom one meets walking across
the quadrangle or going about their business within
its sheltered enclosure, strike absolutely the right
note, and fill one with a sense of the fitness of things,
human as well as architectural.

Some of the brothers wear long black gowns and a
large silver cross upon their breasts. This uniform
was first adopted about 1135 under the founder,
Bishop Henry de Blois. This same Henry de Blois
would seem to have been a genial and interesting
character. He was the fourth son of Stephen,
Count of Blois, half-brother of King Stephen, and
therefore a grandson of William the Conqueror. Not
only was he an ecclesiastic—becoming Bishop of
Winchester at the age of twenty-eight and ruling the
see for forty-two years—but, like many of the old
Norman churchmen, he was a warrior as well.

We are told, too, that he was much interested in
birds and beasts, of which he had a large collection

at Wolvesey Castle, and that he had, as well, a great taste for all forms of art. He collected many kinds of jewels, gems, embroideries, and statuary, and with them he made beautiful and enriched his noble home.

In those early days, surely, such likings show unusual discrimination and culture.

When an old man, his eyesight failed, but his unstinted charity did not, for we read that sometimes his open-handed generosity left him with barely enough to maintain his household and himself.

He erected St Cross to shelter "thirteen poor men, feeble and so reduced in strength that they can hardly, or with difficulty, support themselves without another's aid." They were to be provided with "garments and beds suitable to their infirmities, good wheaten bread daily of the weight of five marks, and three dishes at dinner and one at supper suitable to the day, and drink of good stuff."

Gradually, however, the Hospital fell upon evil times, and all manner of abuses were practised. To the famous William of Wykeham is due the merit of having fought for seven years to redeem the institution from its evil plight. At length his efforts prevailed, and he appointed John de Campeden as master. This proved a most wise choice. After five years' leadership Campeden died, and was buried within the church. A splendid brass inside the chancel rails marks his resting-place. The brass, by the way, is one of the most cherished treasures of St Cross. The brother who showed me round proudly drew my attention to it, and boasted that there was not a single scratch on the metal surface, though it was more than five hundred years old.

Later, Cardinal Beaufort, who succeeded Wykeham, planned a new foundation, which he called the Almshouse of Noble Poverty. His almsmen wear maroon gowns and beef-eater hats of the same colour, and, instead of the silver cross, an oval silver badge.

To the right of the Beaufort Tower is the Hundred Mennes Hall, of which I have spoken above. It is a fine old chamber, and has been mercifully preserved to us to this day in the perfection of its structural beauty. Its dais, at which the great folks sat, and the refectory tables on either side for the poor brothers, made me long to peep into the past and watch a meal in progress. The raised hearth in the centre of the room, the musicians' gallery above, and the lofty open roof, still showing the original beams, all combine to form a picture which is quite delightful. A lattice-work fifteenth-century staircase, with its newel surmounted by the carved figure of a pelican—now, alas! headless—leads up to the founder's room over the Beaufort Tower.

Amongst other objects of interest in the old hall, I was attracted by a glass case containing the ancient leather jacks used in Cardinal Beaufort's time, as well as his candlesticks and salt-cellars. On the dining-table stands his beaker and the dinner-bell used when the inmates were summoned to fetch their rations.

I was bidden to ring this, and it gave forth a sonorous call. How it must have gladdened the brothers on " gaudy " days, as the festivals were called ! We read that at these times the brothers had " extraordinary commons." Amongst other delectable dishes they feasted on—

" A sirloin of beef roasted, weighing forty-six pounds and a half, and three large mince-pies, and plum broth, and three joints of mutton for their supper, and six quarts and one pint of beer extraordinary at dinner, and six quarts and one pint of beer after dinner, by the fireside."

Beyond the Hall lie the almshouses. In these each brother has his own little domain consisting of three rooms. There are now twenty-eight occupants—twenty-seven brothers and one nurse.

To the left of the quadrangle is the ambulatory, or cloister, a charming building dating from the sixteenth century. It was partially erected by Henry Compton, one of the masters. He afterwards became Bishop of London, and we are told that he crowned William and Mary. An oriel window bears the inscription: "Henry Compton, Episcopus."

Above the ambulatory runs a long low gallery, once the old infirmary. The two form a most attractive structure, and the gallery, a portion of which is almost domestic in style, suggests cosy and homely possibilities, even in those days, for the housing and care of the sick. Involuntarily one pictures, flitting between its arches, the white-coiffed nuns who are said to have inhabited it and tended the brothers in days gone by. From the infirmary a window with a shutter opened into the north transept of the church. This enabled the patients to hear divine service. But now the infirmary is closed and the brothers are nursed in their own rooms.

The Church of St Cross adjoining the ambulatory is a most impressive mass, and fills one with a sense of its solid dignity. Almost every type of architecture may be found there, from Late Norman to debased Renaissance. The whole place is, indeed, a perennial attraction to students, its countless details being luckily in almost perfect preservation.

As to the interior, there are so many interesting features that it is quite a problem to name them briefly.

Here in the north transept, to begin with, is a rounded window with the bird's-wing moulding, while others in the church show the double dog-tooth design. I was awed by the mighty Norman columns. They are tremendous. Their gigantic bulk almost takes away one's breath. My guide declared they are fourteen feet in circumference and ten feet in height, from the base to the capital. Then there are the ancient tiles, quite undamaged, and nearly six hundred years old. They have been relaid, and bear, in some cases, the device, " Havy Mynde." Perhaps the warning may have helped to safeguard them !

An ornate Gothic screen, dating from the fifteenth century, divides the chancel from the Morning or Lady Chapel. Here hangs an interesting triptych, which introduces a strange foreign element. It is the work of Jan de Mabuse, a Flemish painter of the sixteenth century.

The pediments of several of the pillars are sculptured with the forbidden fruit, a lily, the water-plant, and the palm. Tradition—as interpreted by the brother aforesaid—declared these emblems to stand for temptation, purity, baptism, and victory.

The lectern in particular fascinated me. It represents an eagle with outstretched wings and colossal claws, and is carved in wood. The bird's head, however, is declared to be that of a parrot, and on it is placed a heart. Popular theory says this odd combination was intended as a suggestion that the words should come from the heart and not be repeated parrot-fashion.

An adjacent church, that of St Faith, was burnt down in 1509, and some delicately carved woodwork was brought from there to St Cross, as well as the Norman basin of the old font, standing on a pedestal of more recent date.

The church owes to the late Mr Butterfield various improvements made in 1860. I could not but deplore, however, that he chose such a flamboyant colour-scheme for its redecoration. Certainly the crude greens, reds, blues, and yellows are anything but an embellishment to the beautiful sculpture.

St Catherine's Hill

. St Cross .

Behind St Cross and the precincts of the Hospital lies the Home Park with its alluring water meadows. Through these winds the Lock Burn, a tributary brook of the river Itchen. Beyond is the quaintly decorative hill of St Catherine. Amongst the crest of trees on the summit is a maze, one of the few now remaining in England. In the Middle Ages they were to be found on many a village green. Hampshire still possesses two, and in that county they are honoured with the local name of Miz-maze. The maze on St Catherine's Down, cut in the chalk, is square. The other on Breamore Down is circular.

I would willingly have loitered in the old quadrangle, where long shadows were beginning to creep across the grass; but the westering sun warned me that time waits for no woman, so I walked regretfully along the broad gravel path towards the entrance gate.

One of the brothers of the Noble Poverty was passing, and wished me good afternoon. The chance seemed heaven-sent, for I had been consumed with a longing to jot down one of these picturesque figures in my sketch-book. So, greatly daring, I proffered my request. It was met with smiling consent; in fact, Brother Douglas seemed only too pleased to stand for me, and here is the result.

As I walked back to the station I remembered that Winchester is the Wintoncester of Thomas Hardy's great novel, *Tess of the D'Urbervilles*. Here was enacted the final scene of Tess's tragic life. Gazing

up at the "ugly flat-topped octagonal tower" of
the prison, imagination sent the black flag—sinister

M.F.R.

Brother Douglas —
S⁺ Cross.

signal of Tess's death—slowly fluttering anew to the
summit of the staff. . . .

What a wonderful book! But Tess's death always
saddens me. I dismissed the thought, and returned
instead mentally to the peace of St Cross. The few

sunny hours I had spent there might almost have
been passed in some remote land, far from the bustle
of everyday life—a land where the quiet old folk
awaited their call to an unknown realm still more
remote.

GOD'S HOUSE, EWELME

THERE is a bosky village in Oxfordshire which holds a jewel of great worth. A clear stream wanders under the leafy elms and gives its name to a cluster of old cottages that clamber up the rising ground capped by an ancient and most beautiful church. This church is attached to a group of almshouses, and the stream is the Newelme, or Ewelme, of which the early meaning is said to be the spring.

William de la Pole, Duke of Suffolk, and the Duchess Alice, his wife, were responsible for the erection of the church, and this great lady was a granddaughter of our poet, Geoffrey Chaucer. They were, it would seem, an ideal couple. But their bliss was short-lived, for though esteemed by his king, Henry VI, a weak monarch withal, Duke William fell a victim to political intrigues and got into the bad graces of the war party. The luckless nobleman was therefore exiled for five years, and was voyaging to Calais when his boat was overtaken by some ships belonging to his political enemies. He was seized, removed from one vessel to another when far from liege and lady, and, after a mock trial, he was promptly beheaded.

One can imagine the shock that the news of his ill-fated end must have given his duchess !

It was after his tragic death that she also took up matters of State and policy, in which it appears that she mixed not wisely but too well. Towards the end of her life, however, she retired to her " fayre manor of brick and tymbre."

Here, with a determination and thoroughness habitual to her—or so we read—she devoted herself to the maintenance of the group of almshouses owing their foundation to her late husband.

Within the church is to be found her exquisite monument. A carved figure of serene purity wrought in creamy glowing alabaster, she lies there surrounded by the soft folds of her wimple and veil, long slender hands joined in prayer. I wish I could convey to you in words the sensitive refinement, the delicate yet strong spirituality, in that sleeping face. The decorous, dignified folds of kirtle, gown, and mantle fall straightly and simply to her feet, which rest on a crouching lion. Above her head, which is encircled by a ducal coronet, is a richly carved canopy, and on her left arm is the Garter. Yet, looking at that quiet face, so indifferent in its marble calm to all pomp and wealth, one feels these outward and visible signs of her worldly estate to be superfluous.

Great artistry has been expended on the sumptuous carvings surrounding the tomb. Many winged angels and other celestial spirits are crowded about her image, and the stone of which they are fashioned is still brilliantly tinted. One wonders if such lavish ornament could have met the wishes of the woman lying there. No one knows, however, whether the figure is really a reliable likeness of the dead duchess, for I learnt afterwards that a monument almost exactly similar in form and expression is to be found in the village church of Stourton in Dorsetshire.

At any rate, the rest of the Ewelme sanctuary is a perfect setting for her tomb, and we read in Murray's *Oxfordshire* that this exquisite memorial " is certainly not surpassed in beauty or excellence of preservation by any monument in England."

The tomb of the duchess lies between the chancel and St John's Chapel at the eastern end of the south aisle, and it is to this little chapel that the residents of the Ewelme almshouses come daily at ten to worship. Its roof is delightfully and elaborately carved in Spanish chestnut, the main device being the letters IHS. At first sight the sumptuous roofing appears as fresh and perfect as when first completed over four hundred years ago. But I hear, alas! that the authorities have detected portentous signs of lurking evil, the malignant work of an inimical insect, the death-watch beetle, and that steps are to be taken at all costs to check its devastating inroads.

Spanish chestnut seems to have been the favourite wood used in the decoration of this church. The rood-screen — of charming Jacobean design — is fashioned from it, and has slender iron columns bearing traces still of red and blue tints. The door

in the screen works on a marvellous hinge of wood
—a far more perfect contrivance than our rough-and-
ready metal ones of to-day.

The whole building, indeed, is rich in carvings, a
high and very elaborate conical font-cover being one
of its most remarkable examples.

The pillars of the nave are ornamented with
corbels showing for the most part grotesque heads.
One, crowned and more dignified than the rest, is
generally supposed to represent Edward III.

From the church one descends into the old quadrangle of the almshouses, round the four sides of
which run quaint cloisters with penthouse roofs.
When I was there the quadrangle was gay with pots
of homely flowers, and narrow borders were set
with many bright blossoms and flowering shrubs.
An old pump stands in the centre of the square.
The barge - boards of the gabled roofs are finely
carved, and the whole exterior of the dwellings is
most attractive, the brick and timber of the walls
being symmetrically arranged in a herring-bone
pattern.

Within dwell thirteen almsmen in homely comfort,
and they have a nurse and doctor to look after
them; though it is true that they are restrained
by many queer rules and regulations of the early
foundation, two or three of which I feel I must
quote for you.

For instance, "no wood man (crazy person) must
be received." We also read that even the master

himself was "like to be fined" for any fault "after the quality and quantity of his crime."

Miss Clay, in her *Mediæval Hospitals of England,* writes that the fines were inflicted not only upon those who were rebellious or neglected to clean up the courtyard and weed their gardens, but also upon those who arrived in church without their tabards, or were unpunctual. "And if it so be that any of thayme be so negligent and slewthful that the fyrst psalme of Matyns be begon or he come into his stall that than he lose one penny, and yf any of thaym be absent to the begynning of the fyrst lesson that than he lose two pence; And for absence fro prime, terce, sext and nynth, for ich of thayme one penny. Also if any . . . be absent from the masse to the begynning of the pistyll . . . one penny, and yf absent to the gospell . . . two pence."

Industry, punctuality, and regularity must have become necessary virtues, seeing that the usual allowance was but fourteen pence weekly. The amount certainly would not go far in our days; but values have changed since the fifteenth century. Furthermore, the poor men "are not to walk about much within or out of the parish, nor are they to be absent from the almshouse, the church, or the church-yard for longer than an hour unless the master give them leave." The almsman is, besides, to wear "a tabarde of his owne with a rede cross on the breste, and a hode (hood) accordinge to the same." During service he was not to enter the church without them. The priests, of whom two were appointed, were enjoined to be sober and discreet and to avoid quarrelling and gossip.

These rules and regulations, and many more, were shown to me in the muniment room, to which I now repaired. A mighty volume was taken out of a safe for my inspection. In this book the documents with their huge seals relating to the foundation are most carefully bestowed. How I longed for the chance to investigate them in a more thorough fashion than time allowed ! But another book contained three short notes in the handwriting of the Duchess Alice, and these I would not have you pass over. They are written to " Cok of Bylton," her steward.

In one of them she bids him take care of her books left in her closet. The second one is dated from London " in myne Inne." In this letter she enjoins him to send to her by a trusty messenger " her little coffre of Gould," and in the third note she instructs him to pay certain moneys from a bag "lying upon the coffre in my closet," and warns him to " take good hyde (heed) about you, for sherewes ben nyghe."

I lingered in the muniment room until lengthening shadows at last warned me that I dared not trespass longer on the time of the kind vicar who showed me all these interesting things. So I regretfully took my leave.

A few hundred yards below the almshouse I came upon the school building, dating from the same foundation. It is now used as the village school.

I was delighted with the exterior, and, as I was looking at it, two small urchins joined me and stood admiring with me the angels adorning the window heads.   Possibly they had never noticed them before!

Afterwards I enjoyed a cup of tea at the village inn, the Greyhound, and reluctantly left this idyllic retreat.

THE WHITGIFT HOSPITAL, CROYDON

THE county of Surrey, perhaps the most verdant and beautiful of our Home Counties, has the proud privilege of possessing two almshouses, both founded by archbishops of Canterbury. The smaller of the two, John Whitgift's Hospital at Croydon, is also the older, and, being the nearer to hand, I visited it first. The environs of Croydon, alas! are countrified no longer. It is hardly even a suburb now—merely another spoke in the ever-increasing circle of London's mighty wheel.

Whitgift began the building of the place in 1596, and took, we are told, a close interest in the carrying out of the work. Much in the same way, no doubt, one of our greatest architects must recently have lingered lovingly over the fashioning of a royal dolls' house. At any rate, the Archbishop superintended every detail of the Croydon foundation, even to the selection of a text to be carved over the front door, which gave him great pause. Finally he decided on the verse from Prov. xxviii: "Qui dat pauperi, non indigebit."

The good man had the cause of the almshouses very much at heart, and was terribly anxious that

the building of the place should be completed during
his lifetime, so that, as Stowe writes, " he would
not be to his executors a cause of their damnation,
remembering the good advice that an ancient father
hath left written to all posteritie: ' It is a way far
more safe for a man to do good and charitable deeds
by himself while he liveth, than to hope that others
will do the same for him after his death.' "

Whitgift's Hospital of the Holy Trinity, therefore,
was fairly " founded and builded of stone and brick
for the relief and sustentation of certain poor people."
Like the Dolls' House, the Whitgift Hospital has
become " a notable and memorable monument," and
both, we must hope, will remain with us enduringly.

The Hospital was finished in 1599. Before and at
its birth so much anxious care had been spent on its
fashioning, that one would think a just fate would
equalise things by blessing it with a peaceful and
serene existence afterwards. Facts, however, indi-
cate the contrary. For Croydon's Holy Trinity has
only escaped total annihilation by the skin of its
teeth, so to speak.

Several zealous but misguided people banded
themselves together, and, on the plea of progress
and commercial expediency, appealed for the demolition of the Hospital. This would, they said, facilitate
the widening of the streets in its neighbourhood.

The reasons for the continued existence of the
Hospital were movingly set down by Mr John Drinkwater in a prefatory note to a protest published at

the time. And it would seem that, at any rate for the present, the destructive scheme has been set aside. Possibly the counsels of those who reverence tradition and beauty will prevail—" a beauty," as Mr Drinkwater writes, " that is ours from wise and loving hands of old."

When once Whitgift had brought the little Hospital into being, he seized every available chance to take refuge in it from the stressful life of responsibility at Lambeth. The rooms that were kept for him remain as far as possible untouched—the oak panelling, reaching from floor to ceiling, is indeed a joy to the eye. A hidden door leads up by a steep, winding staircase to his bedroom, strongly guarded by another door—nine panelled this, with locks concealed in the studs. It looks, indeed, as if Whitgift was taking no risks, as we say nowadays, and who shall blame him for his caution? It was a time of factions and alarms, and men holding prominent positions often went in fear of their lives, so that our founder must have had many a bad quarter of an hour.

He loved to dine among " his poor brethren," as he called them, and often managed to do so after Queen Elizabeth had honoured his table at Lambeth, or so we are told by Isaak Walton. Perhaps he liked to show that he could take a leaf out of her book, and that condescension was not only a Royal quality.

The queen set great store by Whitgift, who was one of the most learned of the Reformed archbishops.

His reputation as a preacher was so great that she commanded him to preach at Court. She nicknamed him her "little black husband," and she would often say she pitied him because she trusted him. It is even recorded that she would never eat flesh in Lent without obtaining a licence from him.

When I entered the quadrangle of the almshouse I could understand the attraction it exercised over its maker. It is attractive still in its neat, orderly greenness, bounded by the tiny houses of the pensioners. After the busy roads outside I felt a sense of relief when I found my way into that grassy, quiet space that, until a hundred years ago, by the bye, was a flowery garden.

Next to it and opposite are now gay shops displaying exuberantly the latest fashions in gowns and millinery. Greengrocers' stores, prismatic with every variety of fruit and vegetable, confectioners' shops, exhibiting the most tempting dainties—all these emphasise by contrast the dignity of the Hospital's inscrutable brick front.

Not that somnolence prevailed within, the morning I was there. Far from it. For it was pay-day —the most active time in the week, and all the dear old people in their tidiest and best attire were waiting their turn at the office to receive their usual stipend.

A courtly old chap in his Sunday coat moved aside to let one of the sisters pass in before him. She was a smiling, cheery dame with a velvet cape and bejetted bonnet.

" Ladies first ! " he said to her.

When the business was over the secretary took me to the chapel, a plain, unostentatious building, where I chiefly noticed cavities for lighted tapers at the ends of the ancient benches.

From the wall an authentic portrait of the founder, in full white lawn sleeves and close-fitting cap, looked down upon me. His trim pointed beard is confined by an Elizabethan ruff.

Afterwards I went into the common hall, where the original woodwork and great oak tables still remain. A buttery hatch connects the hall with the kitchen, now used as a washhouse. Somehow this vast place seems dolefully conscious of having fallen from its high estate. In a dark corner gapes the huge open fireplace, almost like a hungry mouth. Perhaps it is craving for the vanished flesh-pots of Elizabethan times, that emitted such fragrant and appetising odours in days gone by.

A narrow oak staircase leads to the first floor, where above the common hall is the audience chamber—very attractive in its low panelled length. Here, besides an interesting carved overmantel and the old Maundy benches, is a very rare and venerable Bible—a great treasure—of which only two or three copies exist. It was proudly displayed for my benefit, and I was allowed reverently to turn the leaves. It is called a " Tryacle " (treacle) Bible, because in Jer. viii, 22, where the usual phrase, " Is there no balm in Gilead ? " occurs, the words

" tryacle in Gilead " have been printed instead. In the same volume, in Judg. ix, 53, I happened upon the quaint passage, "And a certaine woman cast a piece of a millstone upon his head and all to brake his braine-panne."

On the wall in this room two old pictures attracted me. One is a signboard belonging to the Swan Inn, which, in former days, stood near to Whitgift's Hospital. The picture claims to have been painted in the fourteenth century, but if so, it has certainly been lavishly restored since then. Personally, I cannot quite credit its antiquity. The design impressed me as far more recent. The other canvas is by an artist called Pyne. The subject is North End, and it depicts the Hospital a hundred and fifty years ago.

An old Armada chest stands at the end of the room, and was, I heard, crammed with ancient and interesting documents relative to the foundation; and above it, in a glass case, hang some most notable deeds with weighty seals appended—one of them that of the Virgin Queen herself.

The almshouse used to contain two old mazer bowls, but when the building was threatened with demolition they were removed for safety, my informant believed, to the South Kensington Museum.[1]

---

[1] The origin of the name—mazer bowl—came, I was given to understand, from a combination of maple—the wood of which these bowls are usually made—and meazles—the spotted appearance of that wood !

The bowls are rare objects in our days, though I have come across one or two in my journeyings, notably the fine specimen at King Edward's Almshouses at Saffron Walden, and the one at St Nicholas', Harbledown.

When I left the Whitgift Hospital I felt rested and refreshed by my visit. The little place seems a cheery and peaceful oasis—a quiet harbourage that it was comforting to find in the midst of the turmoil of London.

HOSPITAL OF THE BLESSED TRINITY, GUILDFORD

I ARRIVED at the massive gates of the Hospital of the Blessed Trinity at Guildford in a heavy thunder-shower, and was glad of the protection that its beautiful arched gateway afforded me. A peal at the bell was soon answered by the brother on duty for the day, and he directed me to the quarters of the master, who, though busy at the time, very kindly undertook to explain the chief points of interest of the place.

And it abounds in them !

During the Reformation, the dedication to the saints of any building or place of worship was considered idolatry. This explains the name of the Hospital, as well as of that of its sister at Croydon. It will be remembered, that Trinity Hospital was the second almshouse I had come across in Surrey, built and endowed by an Archbishop of Canterbury. It was erected by Archbishop George Abbot, for the " decayed townsfolk " of his native place. He was generously helped in the noble work by his friend, Sir Nicholas Kempe, who was present at the laying of the foundation stone on 6th April 1619.

We first went into the chapel, where, on a high pedestal, stands an old alms-box lavishly furnished with locks. I wondered if they had been added as obstacles to pilfering—there being safety in numbers. Another treasure is a Vinegar Bible. This edition takes its name from a misprint in the Parable of the Vineyard—for which latter word vinegar was substituted by mistake.

Other than these relics the chapel possesses little to comment on, the designs of two ancient stained-glass windows being of no especial merit, though they have been quite erroneously assigned to Albert Dürer.

Hard by is the common hall. Notwithstanding its thirty feet of length, this is a cosy room, for it is panelled almost to the full height of its walls, and has a fine cornice and carved frieze. A comfortable ancient settle is placed near the open fireplace. Here I came upon three or four of the brothers smoking the pipe of peace. One of them seemed very proud of his surroundings, and chimed in eagerly when I admired the old stools, tables, and benches, of which, with all its other original fittings, this room can boast.

Before mounting the stairs to the great chamber, or guest hall, I went along a narrow passage leading to the rear of the dwellings and peeped into the vegetable garden. The recent shower was over and the whole place lay sparkling in the sunshine. The neat rows of future beans and peas, as well as the pansies and Darwin tulips, looked the better for the sprinkling.   To the right is a charming little pavilion, or garden-house, dating from 1682.

Returning, we passed by the buttery—a frequent adjunct—with its hatch and went up into the great hall.   This has an astonishing old carved mantel-piece of oak, very quaint and elaborate in workman-ship.   The design shows the main features of a banquet in Elizabethan times.   The carver, seuer, cup-bearer, and gentleman-usher are faithfully represented, as well as four open-mouthed voracious guests.

Here, too, is a delightful picture of two children and a lady in white in eighteenth-century dress.   It suggests the influence of Reynolds, and is attributed to John Russell, R.A., who was a native of Guildford.

As we crossed the courtyard again to reach the master's quarters, I was greatly attracted by the fine old doors, of which the lunettes are in the form of scallop shells.   The Hospital is rich in these beautiful lunettes, and they are quite a distinctive feature of the place.

After looking into the master's study, embellished with old panelling and wonderful secret cupboards, he led me up a grand staircase of oak, black with age, exquisitely carved in the jewel-and-pearl design, and possessing fine newel posts.   We glanced into the archbishop's bedroom, which the master now occu-pies, and then made our way to the audience chamber.

Here I was struck by a splendid portrait of Sir Nicholas Kempe, the work of Paul Van Sommer, the Dutch artist. It shows the accurate draughtsmanship so often to be met with in the Netherlands School of painting, but in this instance it is combined with a breadth of technique which delighted me.

The general character of the audience chamber produces a great feeling of satisfaction. With its wonderful carved mantelpiece reaching nearly to the ceiling, and its beautiful panelled walls, it gives an impression of absolute harmony. I must, however, except a fine set of Chippendale chairs, whose backs show the honeycomb design. Though admirable examples of that great craftsman's work, they certainly clash in a Tudor room.

From this chamber we went through a double door and up a spiral staircase into the treasury or muniment room. Here the Duke of Monmouth was brought to spend a night on the way to London, after his capture at Sedgemoor.

" Some say," the master remarked, " the duke slept here, but under the tragic circumstances, I must own that slumber of his seems to me very doubtful ! "

The muniment room contains three chests holding documents relating to the foundation. One of these chests is indeed a mysterious receptacle with its many locks, the centre one being of Gothic design. The hinges of another coffer represent cocks crowing lustily.

As we passed through the audience chamber again,

the master pointed out to me a door known as the Sub-Rosa door. On it is carved a Tudor rose, and under this was formerly an aperture used as an observation panel. The opening has now been boarded up, though its moulding remains, clear evidence of its existence in the past.

After thanking my guide for all his trouble, I

Arms of the Hospital of
The Blessed Trinity
or Abbot's Hospital.
Guildford.
m.F.R.

found myself in the quadrangle again, where the spacious enclosure—it is, in fact, seventy feet square —makes a pleasant picture, for it is tastefully laid out with walks and flower-beds and bedecked with large pots of clipped shrubs. On one side are the men's apartments and on the other side the women's.

As I turned, after leaving it, to look back at the Hospital from the high road, two turrets—one on either side of the central gateway—caught my eye. They are nearly octagonal in shape, and form graceful additions to the exterior of the stately building. There is also the Royal coat-of-arms, and, on high, a large sundial, as well as the Latin inscription, " Deus nobis hæc otia fecit."

No words could better suggest the origin of the happy peace which dominates the place.

LEYCESTER'S HOSPITAL
WARWICK

LEYCESTER'S HOSPITAL
WARWICK

LORD LEYCESTER'S HOSPITAL, WARWICK

No mediæval almshouse that it has been my good fortune to meet with in my journeyings seems more deeply wrapped in romance than Lord Leycester's Hospital, or, as it is often called, the Maison Dieu, Warwick. St Cross at Winchester certainly competes closely with it, but the Maison Dieu, with its charming exterior and its enthralling life-history, surely claims quite as much of one's interest.

To lovers of the romantic its first great appeal undoubtedly lies in the fact that it was founded by Robert Dudley, Earl of Leycester, "Queen Elizabeth's favourite fancy-man," to quote from the guide, a wonderfully virile and original old fellow, who took me round. He, by the way, is one of the long series of old soldiers who, under the provisions of Lord Dudley, have found shelter in the Hospital.

Robert Dudley ! The mere name thrills one, even in these days when thrills are more or less daily matters of course, imbibed with the early morning cup of tea. Unscrupulous and almost recklessly aspiring as we know Leycester to have been, *grand amoureux* as he undoubtedly was, there must yet have been that about his seductive and fearless person which carried him conqueringly over many obstacles and irresistibly commanded admiration.   Indeed, the story of his passionate intrigues and of his many gallantries still fascinates one—intrigues and gallantries which, despite his soaring ambitions as a statesman, he yet found time for, gay buccaneer that he was.

Recalling the stirring events in which he had so large a part, the name of his beautiful and ill-fated wife, Amy Robsart, inevitably recurs to one.   The Hospital can show a priceless survival of her handicraft.   Moreover, from the tower of the little chapel one can catch a distant glimpse of meadows where once Kenilworth Castle stood.   Here, as we know, Amy penetrated to the Royal presence, but was soon hurried back to Cumnor Hall to meet her doomed end.

Only hoary ruins of Kenilworth now stand to remind us visibly of that tragic tale, though it has been most dramatically and romantically perpetuated for us by Sir Walter Scott.   Let me quote the final verse of the old ballad which he transcribed in his novel :

> " Full many a traveller oft has sigh'd
>   And pensive wept the Countess' fall,
>   As wandering onwards they've espied
>   The haunted towers of Cumnor Hall."

Despite Robert Dudley's indiscretions, he must have made frequent *beaux gestes* during his romantic career.   His Maison Dieu was one of them.   Notwithstanding all the vicissitudes of his varied life, he never forgot his Hospital. Through three matrimonial ventures and the changing fortunes of royal favour and disfavour, he still found time and thought to direct the destinies of his generous foundation.

The building, however, has even earlier roots than those he planted. It dates from the reign of Henry VI, and belonged originally to two fraternities, one honouring the Holy Trinity and the Blessed Virgin, and the other St George the Martyr. When these fraternities were dissolved the place became the property of the bailiffs and burgesses of Warwick.

In those days, as we know, the great of the land indulged in the generous practice of founding and endowing charitable institutions, and Dudley, conceiving the notion of giving a hospital to his country, sought and was granted the ground on which to carry out this benevolent purpose. Probably nothing could be refused to Queen Bess's favourite, and in due course the place was made over to him. One can well understand its attraction for its founder, since even now it shows us in large measure the same charming traits that must have conquered him.

Walking up Jury Street, the principal artery of the old town of Warwick, and along High Street— a prolongation of it—one becomes gradually aware of the exquisite little Tudor pile—the apotheosis of

the thoroughfare, so to speak—awaiting one at its
far end. How delightfully each feature of this
timbered fifteenth-century marvel reveals itself in
turn ! Warwick is, indeed, a place of contrasts, for
a few streets away, across the russet-tiled roofs
and swaying tree-tops, stands Warwick Castle, that
Scott calls " the fairest monument of ancient and
chivalrous splendour which yet remains uninjured by
time." The frowning austerity of its turreted heights
contrasts grimly with the delightful, if humbler,
features of the Hospital.

As one walks up Jury Street—the old name is
derived, I read, from a *matted* room in it, where the
juries were impanelled in former times—walking up
the old street then, the tower of the small Early
Norman chapel first comes into view. It is at once
sterner and more rugged in character than the
beamed and plastered frontage of its Tudor neighbour, which displays all the amenities of the enchanting domestic architecture of the period.

Fantastic as the notion may seem, one can almost
feel that the chapel of St James shows hard masculine
features, while the little Hospital, nestling so coyly
at its side, with its gaily coloured coats-of-arms and
the dapper white and black of its timbered face,
appears to smile at one with a coquetry almost
feminine, as if it had put on all its dainty colours
to balance its companion's austerity. The heraldic
emblems of the Dudley family decorate it brightly
with red, blue, and gold. They flank Dudley's

motto, "Droit et Loyal," which, between ourselves,
would seem to protest too much, for the nobleman
was surely neither particularly straightforward with
his wife nor, by the same showing, loyal to his
queen!

In the courtyard cheerful flowers on the window-
sills and balconies light up the old place with their
brilliance.

Then there are the arms of James I—a rose and
thistle—put up to commemorate his visit to the
Maison Dieu in the seventeenth century. Of this
you shall hear more when you visit the big dining-
hall. There also appears repeatedly the well-known
badge of the Dudley family, the bear and ragged
staff. So ubiquitous is this device and so varied are
the attitudes—there are six of them—in which the
furry beast is shown, that one almost imagines it
must have broken loose in earnest, thereby giving
its keepers an opportunity of studying its poses and
of perpetuating its uncouth gambols.

The interior of the building abounds with quite as
many relics as the exterior. The old kitchen has
been turned into a sort of museum, and here are
housed several interesting things. There is an
ancient Saxon chair a thousand years old, and over
it hangs some beautiful stitchery, the work of Amy
Robsart, of which I have spoken before. It is part
of a curtain embroidered by her and brought from
Cumnor Hall.

Near by stands an antique and elaborately carved

wardrobe, which came from Kenilworth Castle, and
was a gift from Leycester to Gloriana. It is not the
only memento of the founder, for there are, besides,
some words in his handwriting framed above his
signature.

The museum holds, as well, a goodly show of ancient
weapons, helmets, and the like of all periods, and a
huge bullet, as large as a football, picked up on the
battlefield of Edgehill. I was shown, also, some old
muskets given to the brothers to defend the Hospital
at the time of the Chartist agitation.

" But they didn't have to use them," said my
guide ; " they just poked them over the walls and
the mob ran away ! "

He spoke with so much assurance that one felt,
in some previous incarnation, he must certainly have
witnessed the whole scene.

I noticed several mugs and goblets, and could
picture the old soldier-brothers grasping them and
tossing down with gusto, on thirsty summer days,
welcome draughts of home-brewed mead.

On the opposite side of the quadrangle is the dining
or banqueting-hall, now, it is true, no longer complete, for the musicians' gallery was incorporated with
the master's house some hundred and fifty years ago.
The raftered roof of Spanish chestnut appears as
new as it must have looked when first put up. This
fresh quality, by the way, would seem to be characteristic of the wood. Some vestiges of carved corbels
are still to be seen. Arresting, too, is a panel which

sets forth in large painted letters a "Memorandum
that King James the First was right nobly enter-
tained at a supper in this hall by the Hon. Sir Fulke
Greville, Chancellor of the Exchequer and one of His
Majesty's most Honourable Privy Council, upon the
4th day of Sept. Anno Dom. 1617.   God Save the
King."

I realised to what base uses adversity may turn the
noblest survivals when I was shown, in this fine old
banqueting-hall, a number of rough wooden cubicles
where the brothers keep their coal !   A large mangle
further testifies to the plebeian practices now in vogue
there—greater contrast still with past pomp and
circumstance.

A master and twelve brothers are housed at
Leycester's Hospital, and the wedded amongst them
are allowed the company of their wives.   But my
guide laid emphasis on the fact that "this is a man's
place," so if a married brother dies, his widow is
obliged to seek other quarters.   No doubt, therefore,
many affectionate and careful wives live in double
dread of their partner's death.

I was then taken to the chapel over the "Hongyn,"
or west gate of the town.   Passing along a raised
stone pathway that threads the flying buttresses—
additions more recent than the ancient exterior—we
entered the little place of worship.   Though very
much restored in 1863 by Sir Gilbert Scott, to whom
it certainly owes a handsome screen and some well-
fashioned stalls, it dates back to its original founder,

Roger of Newburgh (1123), and an old-world spirit still seems to haunt the quiet little place.

Leaving it, we stood gazing down the road. Gay char-à-bancs passed us, full of tourists both English and American, for Warwick is a favourite haunt of our cousins from across the herring-pond. I must confess that the latter-day clamour rather jarred on my sense of the fitness of things, but the bustle seemed in no way to come amiss to my old guide.

" We're lively here at times, as you see, ma'am," he said; " but I like a bit o' life. Give a guess at my age," he suggested to me.

I hazarded, " Seventy-two," for though rather stiff in the joints, the game old fellow had a lusty and gallant way with him.

" Seventy-two ! " He grinned. " Ah, you little know ! If I live and well come next September, I shall be eighty-five."

I marvelled at his toughness, and told him so.

" You negotiate these stone steps much better than I do," I remarked.

" That's because I've always kept going and always shall, as long as the good God gives me life. I can scrub down the floors and stairs for my wife as well as I scrubbed the tables and blackleaded the grates when I was in the army."

" Well, I think it's awfully good of you to have given me so much of your time," I said in farewell, as I offered him my small gratuity.

" Oh, don't you thank me for that, ma'am. I

always treat rich and poor alike. That's my disposition ! I hope Heaven will send you health and
that you'll live for many years."

So virile was his personality that I felt some of his
buoyancy had entered into me, despite the languor
of the rather depleting Warwick air.

Passing along the front of the Hospital on my way
out, I noticed a brother of quite a different type.
Tall beyond the average, and bearing himself with
a dignity that was almost ceremonious, this old
man's figure drew my attention at once.   I pictured
him, sword at hip and cape on shoulder—stripped
of his everyday twentieth-century clothes, and
garbed instead in black trunk hose and doublet,
starched ruff and cap with a sable plume—and there
would stand, to the life, an elderly Elizabethan
courtier.   I guessed that this must be the brother of
whose skill as an engraver on glass I had happened
to hear.   Rather hesitatingly I ventured to speak to
him.

He smiled down at me in confirmation of my sur-
mise.   There was, I assure you, more than a hint of
benevolent condescension in that smile.

" Perhaps, madam, you would honour me by
coming into my rooms ?   I will show you some of
my work."

He ushered me into his dwelling, where, ranged
on shelves, were goblets, glasses, bowls, chalices,
carafes, and decanters of all sizes and all kinds.
On these he had made it his work to engrave, skilfully

and delicately, many subjects. There were birds in flight, there were spreading peacocks, there was Reynard with the hounds in full cry after him, there were butterflies and flowers.

He handled the fragile things with the love of the creator as he passed them to me.

" I'd be very glad at any time to carry out any orders for you, madam," he said, pointing out a graceful monogram on a wineglass. " When Princess Mary married we sent her a goblet. I had been privileged to engrave her monogram on it, and she was graciously pleased to accept our gift."

I promised to do what I could for him, and feel, indeed, that his work merits notice.

On the Sunday I was at Warwick I saw all the brothers assembled reverently in church in the full panoply of beef-eater hats and long-sleeved black cloth gowns. These have floating panels bearing a silver badge that shows the bear and ragged staff. Afterwards the brothers filed out, their quaint garments harmonising well with the mediæval character of the sunlit street.

Before leaving the old town I peeped through the fine wrought-iron gates of a beautiful ancient manor house. It is called St John's, and its history dates from the reign of Henry II, when it was founded for " entertainment and reception of strangers and travailers as well as those that were poor and infirm." Now it has drifted into private hands, and the gates are barred to the curious and the would-be intruder.   So all I could do was to gaze admiringly and a little wistfully at its five gables and its mullioned windows—and pass on.

There are many beautiful and historic landmarks in the old place, and I am sorely tempted to dwell upon them, but none can surpass in beauty and romance the Maison Dieu of Robert Dudley.

FORD'S HOSPITAL, COVENTRY

There are two admirable almshouses in Coventry, and both are renowned for architectural excellence. A space of only twenty years passed between their founding, so that it becomes hard to know with which to deal first. Ford's Hospital must, however, one supposes, claim one's prior attention, because, Miss Clay tells us, it is " placed in a class by itself." She speaks of it as " a half-timbered house—a perfect gem of domestic architecture."

Mr Heath, too, says that its " west front is probably the most beautiful example of the English timbered house of the sixteenth century we possess."

Only in Chester, I may add, where, as everyone knows, ancient houses abound, have I seen such fine Tudor timber and plaster work.

It seems right, therefore, to visit Ford's first, although Bond's Hospital claims priority in age.

Ford's almshouses have an alias—the Grey Friars' Hospital. The institution was given this name because, in the fourteenth century, the monastery of the Grey Friars, though covering much more ground, stood very near this spot. Even now, in the garden at the back of the building, we can see portions of the ancient walls.

William Ford erected his Hospital in 1529.   He was born in Coventry, and, like so many other benefactors of these charities, he was a merchant of the Staple.

The original endowment was for five poor men and a woman, but to-day it accommodates only women.

The city first provided England with ribbons. Ribbons !   A gay and cheerful commodity that must have endeared the place to the female British heart. From that gaudy produce it passed on to watch-making.   After this it underwent a period of stagnation, until it gauged the coming demand for cycles and motors of all kinds.   Then, actually and meta-phorically, things began to hum, and the universal clamour for this merchandise set Coventry affluently on its feet again.

It is now a busy manufacturing centre, and many changes have been suffered by it in the course of its long history and also by the charity of which it is so justly proud.   And though not of the " sea," these changes, like that of Prospero, have been for the most part into something " rich " if not " strange " !

The summer when I was there I found its narrow streets bustling and noisy.   Through them, searching for the almshouses, I made my way, warm and weary. When at last I reached my goal in retired Grey Friars' Lane, I was proportionately grateful for the quiet charm that faced me.

The old gables with their elaborately carved barge-boards and the three projecting groups of latticed windows beneath them are enchanting.   I stood for a

while in the refreshing shade they cast and examined
them at my leisure.   The exterior and the wood used
in its fashioning have been but little restored, and
the whole thing is beautiful and decorative.

A delightful old doorway embellished with small
groups of carved beams, and showing delicate relief

Doorway - Ford's Hospital
Coventry

work over its arch, leads through a passage to a long
narrow court, thirty-nine feet by twelve feet, and on
to this the dwellings open.

Every door is adorned with a different design, and
each window-frame varies in some degree from its
neighbour.   In front of the windows along the
ground floor were—when I happened on them—a
lengthy row of flower-pots, and the geraniums, pinks,
mignonette, stocks, and fuchsias blossoming there

FORD'S HOSPITAL
COVENTRY

BOND'S HOSPITAL, BABLAKE
COVENTRY

struck just the requisite note of colour amongst the black of the old oak and the cream of the plaster.

At the entrance of the passage-way is a tiny room in which services are held. By a small and devious staircase I ascended to an upstairs room, where some ,fragments of old glass foster the notion that the place was formerly used as a chapel.

From the opposite end of the court the almsmen's gardens are gained. Thence I was taken down into the basement, where I saw a number of cells, now converted into coal-cellars. These—or so several well-instructed visitors have suggested to the· matron —were most probably the cells of the monks in the earliest times of the foundation.

Having done the honours to the best of her ability, my guide, heaping Ossa upon Pelion, invited me into her sitting-room. It was a cheerful little room, and I noticed there, among other articles of *vertu*, two elaborately worked pictures, done in wool, by one of the inmates. Their possessor was justly proud of these works of art, and my special attention was drawn to the shading of a blue velvet cloak in one of them. It is worn by an Egyptian potentate, por- traying Pharaoh, or so I was told, the subject of this piece being Joseph and his Brethren. Certainly the sumptuous texture of the velvet and the jewels in Pharaoh's head-dress have been rendered with a skill that almost amounts to alchemy—in embroidery. The achievement in this homely medium seems to me as amazing as it must have been painstaking.

BOND'S HOSPITAL, COVENTRY

LET me now pass from Ford's to Bond's Hospital in Bablake, Coventry.

It was founded in 1509 by Thomas Bond, a benevolent and wealthy silk mercer of the town.

To all outward appearance the building presents the same aspect as it must have done in that day, so artistically has it been restored. Though not so strikingly picturesque as Ford's, it resembles it in many ways.

Its diamond-paned windows, some with oriel projections, are decorated with tracery, while its gables are elaborately ornamented with carvings and heavy mouldings.

At the present time it houses eleven old men, though originally, *vide* Leland, it was " builded for thirteen poore Folkes."

There are now also many out-pensioners, and their lines are indeed fallen in pleasant places, for the whole bedehouse is most scrupulously clean and is polished till it shines again. Many are the well-thought-out little devices planned for the bedesmen's comfort. So that they may not slip, for instance, the steps of the stairs are roughed, and there is a larder with safes, where each old man's provisions are kept.

In Mr Bond's will a clause provides for " a woman to dish their meat and drink," and the matron of to-day, kind soul, cooks individual meals for each inmate, and was busy on her culinary task the morning of my first visit.

The founder left word that his beneficiaries should yearly have the gift of a black-hooded gown. This has been modernised in our day to a gown and bowler hat, duly worn for church parade and on pay-day.

I was taken into some of the rooms, the matron tapping cautiously because, as she whispered to me, " they generally have a nap after dinner." One cheery old man with whom I passed the time of day was too deaf to hear what I said, but nevertheless laughed heartily at the sight of a visitor and shook me by the hand.

I felt what a contrast he offered to a former brother, John Johnson, who, Mr Heath tells us, " poisoned no less than eight of his co-brothers with rat's-bane, in the hope of becoming senior brother of the house. . . . On the death of his eighth victim he was suspected and questioned, whereupon he promptly poisoned himself ! "

At the back of the dwellings each pensioner has his little garden, and in the shade there are benches and a table, where in summer-time the old fellows can sit, smoke, and chat. In inclement weather, however, the spacious common room is in great requisition.

Passing upstairs to the beautiful oak-panelled board room, I noticed on the way some fine massive doors. In this room, by the bye, are two stately examples of Jacobean and Carolean chairs.

Across the quadrangle is the old Bablake Grammar School for boys, built by Thomas Wheatly in 1560. It was formerly a priests' college, but is now used as a museum.

On the first floor is a delightful ambulatory or open gallery, and I was told there is only one other like it —at Much Wenlock in Shropshire. The old beamed rooms of the school are dignified chambers of the period.

A sample of the ancient uniform of the Bablake scholars is preserved in the Museum. With these garments was worn a round cap with a tassel, the coat being something like that of the Blue Coat boys.

I also caught sight of a chin-strap. This instrument of torture was imposed as a punishment on those boys who were guilty of the offence of talking in school. I wondered whether, since those days, the authorities have found it necessary to inflict a similar penance on girl-scholars!

The Museum and Hospital together possess many attractions, which kindred institutions less well endowed may indeed envy.

ST MARY'S HOSPITAL, CHICHESTER

MUCH had been said to me in praise of St Mary's Hospital, Chichester, which was founded by William the Dean about 1158. I was told it was unique. In fact, only one like it in construction now exists— the Hospice of the Heiligengeist in Lübeck, North Germany.

But in spite of the pæans of admiration to which I had listened, I must own I was unprepared for the really amazing sight of the interior of St Mary's.

So grandly unfamiliar is its aspect, that I almost believe the founder must have intended to surprise all who enter it by the sudden vision of this beautiful building.

Three principal types of hospitals or almshouses are to be found in England. The first is the Leper or Lazar House, or several of which I shall speak. A second is the Collegiate foundation, a cluster of buildings grouped round the chapel and common hall, as at St Cross, Winchester. The third is the Infirmary and House of Call. Of this last, St Mary's Hospital, Chichester, is an instance.

The first impression it gives is of dignified spacious-ness. It is as if one were entering a church rather

63

than a benevolent institution—a church that has cubicles or small dwelling-rooms on either side.

The same splendid roof with open timbers spans the entire length of the wide and lofty edifice. It was originally built with four bays, that still exist. But much later, in 1680, eight fireplaces, with huge brick chimneys in four stacks, were added, one of them carrying the date.

A stone-paved passage runs down the centre of the structure, and each apartment has its own front door. One may guess how greatly the dear old folks cherish this privacy ! On each side of these doors little out-houses have been added that are used as sculleries.

Eight old ladies now live within the walls of the Hospital and four married couples outside. The foundation has been modified several times. "Originally," we read in the late Rev. J. Cavis-Brown's brochure, *An Old English Hospital*, "it was for a Warden and Brothers and Sisters serving God in it, and their chief work consisted in relieving the sick and poor."

In 1528, William Fleshmonger, Dean of Chichester, reorganised the fund, and it then provided for five poor aged brothers and sisters. Afterwards, in the reign of Elizabeth, the constitution was again altered —the casual element was done away with and only aged and infirm persons were received.

Mr Cavis-Brown tells us that " the business of the Hospital was to provide for them (the inmates) in things spiritual and temporal, and especially to secure them a quiet home for the remainder of their days."

Each female pensioner now gets ten shillings every two years, in lieu of a new gown, and each male twelve shillings. Besides this, they are allowed two hundred bundles of wood and two tons of coal.

As originally planned, the old folk were able to listen to the service while lying in their cubicles, for the chapel is only divided from the hall and its little

M F Raphael

miserere Seat,
St Mary's -
Chichester

rooms by an exquisite decorated screen, certainly one of the most beautiful that I have seen.

I now passed into the house of prayer. Its ancient stalls with their miserere seats attracted me at once, and I would gladly have given them a lengthier inspection than I was able, for the carving of each one shows a different subject. There is, too, a fine sedilia with canopies that are most delicately designed, and the piscina is in the same style. I noticed besides that the pews here have holes for holding tapers, a contrivance I have also met with

at the Hospitals of Harbledown and Croydon, as well
as elsewhere.

The custodian pointed out to me that the huge
cross-beams are somewhat worn in places. This, he
explained, had been caused in former days by chains
passing over them. From these the braziers for
heating the place were suspended. This seems a
somewhat primitive method to our twentieth-century
notions—spoiled as we are by central-heating coils
and electricity ! One would think that the risk of
fire in such a beautiful old place must have been a
constant nightmare to the inmates in former times.

As I walked through the hall again I noticed
several large signed photographs. Amongst these
were two of King Edward and Queen Alexandra, when
they were Prince and Princess of Wales, and more of
a later date, after they had come to the throne.

The custodian told me that King Edward had
twice visited the Hospital. The second time, the
king had entered each apartment and chatted with
its owner. One old lady into whose room I was
invited boasted proudly that her Sovereign had
shaken hands with her. As I was leaving, she
switched on the electric light with great satisfaction.
It is a recent and much esteemed addition to the
comfort of the residents.

When my visit to the interior of the Hospital
was concluded, I was taken round the garden to
be shown a blocked-up doorway placed low down
in the north wall. Only the top of the arch is above

ground, and I gathered that this portion had been laid bare when the level of the ground was lowered, for in bygone times the doorway gave access to a subterranean passage leading to the Priory, a couple of fields away. What mysterious and romantic possibilities such a passage suggests !

In this Priory the Friars Minor established themselves in 1253, being forced to move from their former abode, which was then converted into the Hospital of St Mary.

The Priory must have been a fine old building, though it is now, alas, little more than a shell. At the present day it apparently only serves as a glorified garden-shed or storehouse. Most of its windows are bricked up, but I could see, through one or two of them, a stack of seats and other garden accessories. The ruin stands in what is at present called the Priory Park. When I was there an eager crowd was thronging to the grounds, bent on witnessing a football match which was shortly to take place.

From Priory to football ground . . .

A significant reminder that the times change—and we with them.

SACKVILLE COLLEGE, EAST GRINSTEAD

" I PRAY God bless my Lord of Dorset and my Ladie
and al their posteritie.   Ano. Do. 1619."

I read these words over the daintily carved rood-
screen of the chapel in Sackville College, a charming
group of almshouses founded by the second Earl of
Dorset for poor men and women, as set forth in his
will dated 1609.

A portrait of him in oils shows a bearded, stout,
benevolent-looking man in richly embroidered velvet
coat, with cavalier hat and lace-edged linen collar
of the period.   A contemplative, deliberate sort of
man he seems.   Not one who would carelessly scatter
wealth broadcast, but one who would mature his
charitable schemes and then convert them into
systematised widespread liberalities.

His portrait set me thinking how full the world
must have been of the milk of disinterested human
kindness even in those days before organised charity
became a national practice.

The approach to Sackville or Sauqueville College,
as one sometimes finds it spelt, takes one by surprise.
From a humble wicket-gate a diagonal path leads
sheer across an upward slope of grassy sward to the

Sackville College. East Grinstead.

entrance. It was late in the afternoon when I crossed the outer garden enclosed by high chestnut trees breaking into leaf. Their long indigo shadows were creeping with slow persistence over the warm turf. Above the door I noticed an old sundial, whose function for the day was at an end, for the sun had long ago deserted the ripe russet bricks of the ancient façade.

The smiling matron, in her pretty white coif and long navy blue cavalier cloak lined with purple, came to meet me, and we went together into the chapel. She showed me the seat occupied by the warden within the rood-screen, and explained that the honour of sitting next to him fell to the brother longest in residence. She then displayed with much pride the treasures in the chancel—an ambry with an old carved door, and a small Elizabethan chalice delicately wrought in silver and quite perfect of its kind. With bated breath I was cautioned " on no account to touch."

High up on the right wall I noticed a small quatre-foil window which gave into an adjacent room, formerly used as an infirmary. Patients lying there were thus enabled to hear the service. The same consideration for them is to be met with in several institutions, such as St Cross, Winchester, and others, and would seem to have survived from monastic times.

The chapel door was closed with an elaborate mediæval key, of such formidable size as almost to remind one of the key of the Baron's kitchen in the pantomime! As to the lock, it is a masterpiece of art, and the workmanship of its mechanism, most intricately wrought, is very beautiful.

Within the quadrangle and facing the main entrance is the wing named Ye Dorset Lodgings, and over the doorway are the Dorset family arms, with the device, " Aut nunquam tentes aut perfice." The motto certainly seems to have borne fruit, for no more perfect achievement in the seventeenth century as to almshouses could have been carried out.

The hall, one of the rooms originally set apart for the founder, is embellished with carvings and furniture of old black oak that would make any collector's mouth water! The large open hearth boasts iron-dogs in the form of mermaids. I have met with this design before and have often puzzled over its origin. Why should these aquatic creatures, who live by, or rather in, water alone, be condemned constantly to face fire and flame—surely the elements most inimical to them?

There is also a fire-back brought from Buckhurst, a former manor house belonging to the Dorset family. This ironwork was cast in a Sussex foundry; for in days gone by there was coal in Sussex, a commodity now declared to have been exhausted long ago.

Above, to the left of the hall, is the musicians' gallery, and, adorning the right wall, I spied two crossed swords. They are called mortuary swords, and came into being to commemorate the execution of Charles I. They have basket handles, and the guard is engraved with the fallen monarch's portrait and various heraldic emblems. Also hanging here is the original copy of the charter.

Besides the hall, Sackville College owns another beautiful room, the common room, formerly called the refectory, that has recently been put into fresh order. It now holds many modern allurements, such as a listening-in set, of which the loud speaker shines forth in all its metal glory against the antique oak background. There is, as well, a table crowded with up-to-date magazines and a drawer full of playing-cards and other games, so that the fortunate inmates are liberally supplied with recreation.

In a glass-topped table in this room are displayed some precious documents, amongst others a love letter from Mary Howard, addressed to a wooer who would seem to have been somewhat recalcitrant. One cannot but picture the writer's distress if she could have foreseen the publicity to which her rather piteous letter would one day be exposed. Has one the moral right, I wonder, even in the interest of posterity, to exhibit such obviously private correspondence ? In this letter, charming in its naïveté, she beseeches " her dere frend's " goodwill and indulgence.

Out in the courtyard in the centre of the roof a graceful turreted belfry catches one's eye. Studying this, I realised that, topping it, is a cat-like figure squatting on its hind legs and clasping a pole with its fore-paws.

" Ah, you're looking at our leopard, I see," said the matron. " That's a feature of the Dorset crest. At one time there was a weather-vane at the top of that pole, in the shape of a mouse. There is a story which pretends that the leopard was a cat, and that when the cat caught the mouse, Sackville College would come to an end."

It seems, however, that the mouse has long since been lost to sight, though it remains to memory dear.

On the left of the courtyard are a dove-cote and an old well. Two ancient tanks bearing delightful designs in lead-work tracery also grace this open space. They are dated respectively 1701 and 1750.

The green quadrangle is intersected by gravel paths, and all over it a flock of consequential pigeons were busy, courting and prinking themselves, or, with an eye to the main chance, snatching up any unconsidered trifle they could find.

My passage through the garden disturbed them at their business, and there was a mighty flutter of wings above my head as I walked away. It gave a touch of homely life to the quiet scene.

ST JOHN'S HOSPITAL, CANTERBURY

THE old city of Canterbury is so rich, both as to its history and its ecclesiastical remains, that I was not surprised to hear of its possessing several ancient almshouses for the care of the aged.

One of these, Eastbridge Hospital, is dedicated to St Thomas of Canterbury, and stands in the centre of the town. Originally, however, it was less of an almshouse than a house of call for the use of pilgrims, and it was established in order to shelter them for one night only on their way to the shrine of the saint.

Another of these outstanding institutions is the Hospital of St John, founded, we are told, in or about the year 1084 by Archbishop Lanfranc, an Italian cleric established by William the Conqueror as Primate of England.

Eadmer, Lanfranc's disciple and historian, says that this almshouse was planned to accommodate a hundred brothers and sisters from the blind, lame, deaf, and sick.

Going down busy Northgate Street, after passing the King's School on the opposite side of the road, I found the ancient group of houses on my left. An old Tudor gateway leads to the green and quiet

oasis round which the Hospital buildings and hoary
church are clustered. Ruined portions are all that
now remain of the first structure, for it seems that
everything was destroyed by fire in the fourteenth
century.

Old Gateway,
St John's Hospital,
Canterbury

The church shows a rounded Norman doorway
and windows, but has, alas, only its south aisle standing. Beyond this, its chief claim to interest is a
queerly shaped font, roughly circular in form, with
two handles, and having a lid chained to it, "to
keep the witches from getting at the water," or so
local tradition says.

Hard by the church are the remains of a wall, where part of another Norman doorway still stands.

At this point the aged sub-Prior joined me, and, though his sight was failing and he was very deaf, he eagerly offered to show me the old kitchen and hall. On the way we passed some palisaded cubicles, and I was pleased to see that, in spite of everything, his sense of humour had remained unimpaired, for he jokingly suggested that these must have been used as pens for the naughty old women !

Within the kitchen I was shown some enormous spits and the metal pins employed for skewering the joints. Here, no doubt, were prepared the annual feasts that regaled the inmates on St John's Day. In connection with this custom, F. Cross and J. Hall, in their book, *Rambles Round Old Canterbury*, quote from one of the ancient registers the cost of some of the curious and interesting items :

" The bill of fare comprised 80 pounds of beef, at 3d. per lb. A calf cost 18s. Two lambs cost the same amount. Three ' coople ' of chicken cost half-a-crown. To wash down these solid comforts the brothers and sisters appeared to have required ' halfe a barrel of beere,' costing 3s. 2d. ; a gallon of ' sacke,' 3s. 4d. ; a ' pottle of claritt and a pottle of white wine,' in all 2s. 8d. ' Beere to make the serving-men drinke that brought meat to our feast,' cost 2d. ' Beere for the kitchen,' cost 4d., and the ' cooke for drissing the dinner ' was paid handsomely—4s. The 'woman that helped in the kitchen' got 6d., and the two ' turnspets,' 8d."

The " spets " they turned are no doubt those of which I have already spoken.

The venerable sub-Prior and I then climbed up a spiral staircase and reached the hall built over the kitchen.   In this chamber he pointed out the long refectory table and benches of rough oak fastened to the floor.   The wide space between them had no doubt been provided so that the brothers, however ample their girth, could be comfortably seated.

Two fine thirteenth-century chests, and another dating from the fourteenth century—a beautiful specimen—stand against the walls.

My guide also brought out for my inspection several old pewter dishes or pittance platters which, he told me, were used on dole-days when the brothers received " something extra."

There were, besides, three old mazer bowls, whose medallions bear the Tudor rose, the sacred monogram IHS, and the Virgin and Child.

A very quaint alms-box attracted my attention. It is in the form of a Roman lamp, and I wondered if it had been used in olden times when the brothers and sisters were sent throughout the country begging for alms.   This custom, I was told, was in existence until the year 1585.

In 1560 Archbishop Parker framed certain orders for the discipline of the Hospital, and those inmates who infringed them were subject to the usual fines and penances; but many of these rules are no longer in force. One of the punishments condemned the offender to sit in the stocks for three days and three nights. So perhaps it is as well that both rule and stocks have been done away with, for the poor old folk in this inclement twentieth century of ours could scarcely weather such rigorous treatment.

After taking farewell of the sub-Prior I passed under the archway again. Its left wing has been annexed by a curiosity dealer, and I caught sight of many tempting things in his shop. Luckily for me, however, the treasures I had seen in St John's had so impressed me, that I was able to resist the allurement of the varied collection visible through the little lattice shop-window as I turned away.

ST NICHOLAS' HOSPITAL, HARBLEDOWN

FROM Canterbury the next afternoon I made my way down a steep and shady road to the old Lazar House of St Nicholas at Harbledown. Already in the early times of its construction the terrible affliction caused by leprosy had been recognised, and charitable people all over the country generously endeavoured to alleviate this suffering by the foundation of leper hospitals.

The nearer I approached St Nicholas', the more evident it became that benevolent Archbishop Lanfranc, who was responsible for the endowment of this Hospital, as well as for that of St John's, Canterbury, had chosen an ideal spot on which to build. Billowing meadows and hop gardens of Kent form the background of the picture in which Harbledown is set. Less than two miles away rise the splendid towers of Canterbury Cathedral. Behind, wood and copse, carpeted with bluebells, stretch down to the foot of the hamlet. Can it be that this woodland has grown up on the site of the once well-known forest of Blean ? Let us assume it and metaphorically remove our shoes from our feet, for the path we tread may be reckoned sacred ground. We are but a

stone's throw from the ancient Pilgrims' Way.   Here,
we read, came Henry II from Southampton.   After
entering the Church of St Nicholas he walked bare-
footed to the Cathedral, and gave in grant twenty
marks of rent to the Hospital for the love of St
Thomas.

To be perfectly truthful, the position of the Pilgrims' Way is a debatable point, but where so many
historical facts are incontestable, one is loth to rob
the neighbourhood of its enchantment, and I for
one liked to picture the many pilgrims treading the
road that wound in front of me.

In Mr J. Duncombe's *History of Antiquities at or
near Canterbury* (1780) we read that—

"The spot where this Hospital is situated has
been remarked as peculiarly healthful ; and it is
well known that herbalists come regularly every
year to collect medicinal plants that grow only on
this particular spot.   Herbaldown was so styled . . .
to distinguish it from the neighbouring hills, or
downs, as yet continuing wild or woody."

A steep flight of steps leads up to the old timbered
gateway.   I passed under it and, following a little
gravelled path, soon came in sight of flower-beds
thronged with tulips and upstanding fragrant wall-
flowers that formed the foreground of the almshouses.   These stretch on each side of a hall or
common room, now converted into a museum.   Facing them, beyond a prettily planned garden, rises
the Church of St Nicholas.   The sun was lighting

up its hoary stone walls and playing across the rich
grass and over the trim shrubs and creeping ivy that
keep its aged face perennially green. The moment
for a snapshot was irresistible. Just as I had finished
taking it, the sub-Prior emerged from his house and
offered to show me round. He is a mine of information, and his intelligent remarks greatly added to my
enjoyment.

The first feature he pointed out to me when we
entered the church was its pavement, sloping down
from the altar to the west door. It was thus constructed, I was told, for the water to flow away when
the church was cleansed, after the lepers had attended
service.

The old columns are interesting in their massive
simplicity. One, dating from Norman times, has a
capital where grotesque little heads are introduced
into a border of foliage. In the chancel, traces of
the rood-loft are quite visible, and the tints of old
frescoes, which originally adorned the walls of the
nave, are in some places fresh.

Here in St Nicholas', too, I again met with taper-
holes in the old pews.

On the left of the porch as one enters is an
ancient staircase, composed of massive blocks of wood.
They are attached by wooden pins to the trunk of a
tree used as a beam. The stairs lead up to the tower,
where four bells hang, the oldest dating back to 1470.

The font, as well, is an object of antiquity. It is
carved from a solid piece of stone, and was fashioned

in the fifteenth century—some say, indeed, even earlier. At any rate, it bears the Unity rose, which, after the Wars of the Roses, combined the Lancastrian and Yorkist emblems.

·Some fragments of glass in the windows, of a delightful golden colour and showing admirably drawn oak leaves, are fascinating when one recalls their great age. Amongst other designs on the glass I noticed the flower we know as the Canterbury bell. I was told that this name was suggested by the bells on the pilgrims' horses.

We now crossed the sunny garden to the Museum, erected on the site of the original old dining-hall. This contains the Hospital's treasures. With great pride the sub-Prior pointed out to me a Norman chest of which the lid is formed of a hollowed tree-trunk.

I saw, besides, some old pewter platters, formerly used by the pensioners, and a pilgrim's leather flask, that no doubt held emergency water from the miraculous well of St Thomas in Canterbury Cathedral.

I greatly admired an old mazer bowl. I had now seen several of these vessels, but at the bottom of this one the engraving of the medallion is particularly fine and delicate. The design shows Guy of Warwick slaying the dragon. J. Duncombe, in his *History* above named, thus describes the episode :

" Guy, Earl of Warwick, saw a ' dragon and lion fighting together in a forest bordering on the sea, as he was returning to Europe from the relief of

Byzantium. He determined to take up the conqueror, and after the lion was fairly spent, Guy
attacked the dragon, and after many hard blows
on his adamantine scales, spying a bare place under
his wing, he thrust his sword in to the depth of
two feet and, with a dreadful yell, the dragon ex-
pired.' "

Another account of the great Guy—one of the
most ancient and most popular of our early heroes
of romance—is as follows :

" His father was Segard, steward of Rohand, Earl
of Warwick. Having fallen deeply in love with
Felice, the fair and accomplished daughter of the
earl, Guy fell into a grievous sickness, but was
recalled to life by a promise of her hand when he
had earned it by knightly deeds. Immediately
he crossed to Normandy, at the great tournament
of Rouen distanced all competitors, and at once
set out into ' far lands,' travelling through Spain,
Almayne, and Lombardy, and gaining the prize in
every tournament. He then returned to England,
but his haughty mistress was still unsatisfied. Once
more he left his country . . . and well-nigh lost
his life through treachery. He next went to Constantinople to save the Emperor Ernis from the
Saracens. . . . The grateful Emperor pressed on
him the hand of his lovely daughter and heiress, Loret,
but Sir Guy tore himself away, and returned, with
many adventures by the way, to his native country.
No sooner had he reached its shores than tidings

were brought of a most portentous dragon then ravaging Northumberland. He hastened to meet the monster, slew him, and carried his head to King Athelstane at Lincoln. The fair Felice had now no scruple to marry the hero. But regret for all the slaughter he had done merely for a woman's love began to seize him, and, after forty brief days of wedded happiness, he left his home in the dress of a palmer to visit the Holy Land . . . after which he returned to England to find Athelstane besieged in Winchester by the Danish Anlaf, of whose army the mainstay was the terrible Colbrand. Sir Guy, still in his disguise, after a prolonged and awful struggle, succeeded in striking off the champion's head. He now visited his wife, all unknown in his palmer's weeds, and then retired to a hermitage in Ardenne. Before his death he sent her parting ring as a token to Felice, and she arrived in time to close his eyes, survived him but for fifteen days, and was buried in the same grave."

One of the noted possessions of St Nicholas' is a curious old alms-box, to which is attached two or three links of a chain. Tradition says that the lepers were wont to stand on the steps at the gateway holding out a long pole. At the end of this was the alms-box into which passing wayfarers—who might be charitably inclined—dropped their donations.

In the sixteenth century the great scholar and reformer, Erasmus, visited St Nicholas' with his friend, Dean Colet, the founder of St Paul's School.

We may presume that the latter gentleman was of a choleric disposition, for when one of the Hospital's most priceless relics—an old leather shoe of St Thomas the Martyr with a jewel set in it—was offered him to kiss, he refused the privilege in language more

The Erasmus Almsbox
at Harbledown. M.F.R

forcible than polite. The mild and peaceful Erasmus, however, performed the salute indicated, and, further to pacify the indignant brother, he dropped a handsome donation into the alms-box, which the irascible Colet had ignored. The shoe has long since gone the way of all old shoes, but the jewel has been set in the bottom of a mazer bowl that was exhibited to me with great veneration. The sub-Prior added that when some " Pauline " boys were shown the relic, they chuckled with glee on hearing of their founder's lapse.

Erasmus' own account of the incident in his *Peregrinatio Religionis* is as follows :

" In the road to London, not far from Canterbury, is a way extremely hollow as well as narrow, and also steep, the bank being on each side so craggy that there is no escaping nor can it by any means be avoided. On the left side of that road is an alms-house of some old men, one of whom runs out as soon as they perceive a horseman approaching, and, after sprinkling him with holy water, offers him the upper leather of a shoe bound with brass in which a piece of glass is set like a gem. This is kissed and money given him. I had rather have an almshouse of old men on such a road than a troop of sturdy robbers. As Gratian (Dr John Colet, Dean of St Paul's, 1505-19) rode on my right hand, nearer the almshouse, he was sprinkled with water ; to this he submitted ; but when the shoe was held out he asked what it meant. And being told it was the shoe of St Thomas, he was so provoked that turning to me, ' What ' (says he), ' would this herd have us kiss the shoes of all good men'? They may just as well offer their spittle to be kissed. . . .' I took compassion on the old man and gave him some money by way of consolation."

My guide now declared that I must not leave Harbledown without visiting the well of the Black Prince. He took me through an idyllic orchard, where apple blossom rioted against the blue sky. We went down over the grass through a little wicket gate, until, set deep in the ground, we came upon a walled-in old spring.

The keystone of the arch over it shows three feathers bound with the motto, " Ich dien," always associated with the Prince. I am afraid, however, that his connection with the well is problematical, to say the least of it. However, let us give romance the benefit of the doubt, for we read in Mr Heath's *Old English Houses of Alms* that after the Battle of Poictiers, " The King and his prisoner, King John of France, passed through Harbledown (19th April 1357) on their way to Canterbury and London. Halting at the Hospital, they would doubtless be offered the relics to kiss, and would probably drink a cup of water from the holy well."

It is certain, moreover, that the water contains curative properties, especially for the eyes, and Miss Clay makes the remark that hospitals were frequently built near healing springs on that account.

What, after all, more likely than that the pilgrims, pursuing their dusty course along the old Pilgrims' Way, should turn in at St Nicholas' and refresh themselves with a draught from the marvellous spring before they approached the spot of which Chaucer wrote :

> " Wete ye not wher stondeth a litel town
> Which that ycleped is Bob-up-and-down
> Under the Blee in Canterbury way ? "

Let us then, as agreed, give romance the benefit of the doubt. Here in Harbledown each ancient stone, each hoary tree-trunk, is steeped in its glamour. It holds a magic to be encouraged, nay, more, to be cherished, in these matter-of-fact and utilitarian times.

THE HOSPITAL OF SS. JOHN, SHERBORNE

In the old town of Sherborne, Dorsetshire, and forming with its beautiful and well-known Abbey the heart, as it were, of the ancient place, stands the Hospital of SS. John.

The cheerful life of the town rushes past the two venerable buildings and the green oasis of the precincts enclosing them. Yet the bustle does not seem to trouble their repose nor disturb the peace with which they watch the movement of to-day. On a notice-board near by I was delighted to see that a merciful dispensation had forbidden the drawing-up of vehicles in front of the Abbey, and as the almshouses are at right angles to the Close, this wise order leaves the view of both unimpeded—a real cause for rejoicing.

Originally, we are told, a hospital of the Order of St Augustine stood here, begun through the generosity of the good townsfolk. The foundation was augmented in 1437 by licence from King Henry VI to Robert Neville, Bishop of Sarum, Humphery Stafford, and others, and was dedicated to St John the Baptist and St John the Evangelist.

The earliest part of the structure now remaining

is the tiny chapel, where prayers are read each morning and evening by one of the old men, who is called the Prior.   Usually the task of showing visitors round the almshouses also devolves on him,

Entrance to SS John's Almshouses - Sherborne . M.F.R.

but as he was out when I called, this duty was fulfilled by another of the almsmen.

The interior, owning a lofty east window, has been judiciously restored, and the more important south window can boast precious fragments of the original ancient glass.   But most of it, unfortunately, has now vanished and has been replaced by clear diamond panes. It is a pity that the old bits seen in this piecemeal fashion are robbed of much of their beauty. Yet this would seem to be the fate of many priceless remnants of ancient glass the world over.

The chapel's greatest treasure is a delightful triptych, probably given by the founder for an altarpiece. One really feels quite a thrill of surprise when one first comes upon it in its British surroundings. It is considered by some judges to be the work of a Flemish artist. Other experts, however, declare that the painter was Cosmo Roselli. At any rate, whoever he may have been, the result he has achieved here is charming, and time has dealt kindly with the pigments used, so that the colours, though mellowed by years, have retained their exquisite freshness.

When closed, the two outer panels show figures of the four Evangelists. They are rather colourless, but technically quite good, though far less interesting than the paintings within. These illustrate five of Christ's miracles—the Resurrection of Lazarus, the Casting-out of the Devil, the Blind restored to Sight, the Raising of the Widow's Son, and the Healing of Jairus' Daughter.

The body of the chapel is resorted to only by men-worshippers, which is a lucky thing, for it would certainly not accommodate more than twelve persons. At the west end is a little gallery set apart for the " women-folk."

A fine perpendicular arch and an old oak screen

separate the chapel from the ante-chapel and outer hall. The far end of this is enclosed by a row of old settles. Here, gathered round a great fire on the open hearth, were clustered some of the aged almsmen, smoking their pipes as convivially as in any village inn. They seemed to have stepped straight out of one of Thomas Hardy's Wessex novels, where one meets them constantly. One of them, a cheery soul of eighty-seven, expressed himself as most satisfied with his lot.

A dignified old man in the uniform of the foundation—a black coat and brass buttons with the bishop's mitre—acted as my guide, and seemed to enjoy the mission. He quite won my heart. We ascended together to the upper regions, where he took me into one of the rooms of the women's quarters. There a venerable dame, who had just returned from her walk, made a brave figure in her scarlet cloak with its gathered cape, her black gloves and black poke-bonnet, its snowy frill framing her lined but smiling face. The bonnet was soon exchanged for a close-fitting little cap of white net, gay with royal blue ribbons. She explained that, when going beyond the town or for a day's outing, the old ladies are privileged to wear ordinary clothes. This chance was seized with enthusiasm, for the sake of variety one can only suppose, for really no garments could be more pleasing than the Hospital's distinctive dress. The dislike to the wearing of uniform, however, is not confined to Sherborne.

The men's dormitories, into which we next went, have lofty beamed ceilings, and appear to have remained unchanged since they were first built in the fifteenth century. The sick-room is waggon-vaulted, the beams of the ceiling curved like the roof of a waggon.

On this floor, too, is the hall for the use of the masters and brothers. It is very lofty, and shows the roof-timbers, which I was told are of moulded oak. Quatrefoils embellish the sides above the wall-plates. The hall has a splendid oriel window that looks down on to the busy street.

The following quaint list of rules relating to the foundation was drawn up in 1788 :

" Whereas this Almshouse was founded not only for the purpose of relieving the bodily wants and infirmities of poor, feeble, and aged men and women, but also for the good of their souls by affording them an opportunity of joining in a regular dis-charge of their religious duties and so preparing themselves for the hour of death and the day of judgment ;

" It was agreed and ordered . . . that for the time to come, prayers shall be said in this Chapel by the Prior, every day from Ladyday to Michael-mas at seven o'clock in the morning before their breakfast and at three o'clock in the afternoon when there are no prayers in the Church. And in like manner from Michaelmas to Ladyday at eight o'clock in the morning, and at two o'clock in the

afternoon.   That the Prior shall deliver to the Master
a list in writing of the names of such persons as
shall refuse or neglect to attend accordingly, unless
they are prevented by sickness or any other circumstances which the Master shall allow to be a sufficient
excuse.   That every person so refusing or neglecting
to attend the worship of Almighty God, or who shall
not strictly observe the rules and orders of the house,
which are to be read to them once in every month,
shall for the first offence forfeit and lose the next
day's ordinary allowance of diet and not be per-
mitted to go out of the house during that day.   And
for the second offence, such person shall be expelled
this house and another poor man or woman shall
be chosen in his or her room."

I take it that no one imperils their stay in this
haven of peace by infringing the laws, though,
looked at in the light of our own less stringent
measures, they certainly have a somewhat arbitrary
tinge.

Across the Close my old conductor pointed out
the Lady Chapel, which lies between the Abbey and
the celebrated King's School of Sherborne.   He told
me that formerly it was part of the school building,
but has now been reincorporated with the Abbey.
He added that he had been butler to two of the
canons, and had slept for many years in the Lady
Chapel before its restoration.

There was a fine complacency about the old fellow
as he stood in the doorway bidding me farewell.

My admiration of the Hospital had called forth gratified smiles. One felt that he reverenced every fragment of the ancient walls and every tradition relating to them, and that he took almost the same personal pride in the place as a great landowner does in his ancestral acres.

SOME ALMSHOUSES IN BRISTOL

I

THE MERCHANT SEAMEN'S ALMSHOUSES

SHIPS and everything pertaining to the sea have an attraction all their own. On my first morning's walk in Bristol I saw a large steamer lying at the quayside, and farther along I was fascinated by a most unusual and romantic object—a fine five-mast sailing-vessel. Its sails and tapering masts dwarfed the funnels of other ships crowded in the harbour, and rose far above the roofs of Bristol's old houses. Those aspiring mastheads shone out, to my thinking, like carved ivory against the blue of the sky.

Near by on St Augustine's Bridge I read with interest an inscription on a tablet stating that— " From this port John Cabot and his son Sebastian sailed in the ship *St Matthew* A.D. 1497 and discovered the continent of America." For this deed Henry VII rewarded them with the sum of £10.

The famous Sebastian Cabot was a citizen of Bristol and became Governor of the Guild of Merchant Seamen—or Venturers, as they are sometimes called.

From the bridge I made my way to the Merchant

Seamen's Almshouses, founded by the Guild in the sixteenth century and rebuilt in 1696. Outside the gates are the arms of the Merchant Seamen. A mermaid on one side seemed to me to be seeking to entice a figure on the other. This I first took to be Pan, as it had goat's legs. I was, however, corrected, and informed that it stood for Father Time !

At present the houses are inhabited by eleven men and ten women. Over the quarters of the chief brother—a kindly and very intelligent captain from the Merchant Service—is a panel on which I read the following verse :

> " Freed from all storms, the tempest and the rage
> Of billows, here we spend our age ;
> Our weather-beaten vessels here repair,
> And from the merchants' kind and generous care
> Find harbour here. No more we put to sea
> Until we launch into eternity,
> Unless our widows whom we leave behind
> Should want relief, they too a shelter find.
> Thus all our anxious cares and sorrow cease,
> While our kind Guardians turn our toils to ease.
> May they be with an endless Sabbath blest
> Who have afforded unto us this rest."

In the captain's room I afterwards saw his certificate of seamanship, framed, and several pictures of vessels in full sail. He told me he had passed forty-seven years at sea, on sailing-ships and steamers, and during the first year of the Great War his ship was chased by the *Carlsruhe* in the Straits of Florida, but happily escaped.

I was also informed that a short time ago a descendant of Cabot had visited the Hospital.

Having given me all the information in his power, he suggested my applying for permission to see the fine hall of the Merchant Venturers near the quay, and by special favour I was courteously admitted to the hall. It was erected in the seventeenth century, and is a magnificent room, having other fine chambers adjoining it. From the walls Queen Anne, by Kneller, and other pictured Royalties, as well as Colston and various Bristol worthies, looked down on me. I greatly admired the cut-glass chandeliers, the beautifully polished dining-table and other furniture.

II

FOSTER'S ALMSHOUSE

Foster's Almshouse, Bristol, was endowed by John Foster, Mayor of the town in 1481. At present it houses two men and twenty-six women. It has a beautiful little chapel with fine old poppy-headed pews and fragments of the original glass. The church is popularly called the Chapel of the Kings of Cologne, and Miss Clay quotes Leland, who says it was built " in the honour of God and the Three Kings of Cologne." She adds: " It is the sole witness in the way of dedication in England to the veneration of the Magi. The title is said to have been the choice of an Abbot of Tewkesbury at the close of the fifteenth century."

These Magi, or Wise Men of the East, Melchior, Caspar, and Balthazar, preached the gospel in Persia, where they died. Their bodies were removed to Constantinople, then to Milan, and finally the bones were carried to Cologne—hence the name.

Outside the chapel are three niches, where once stood the figures of the saints, and below and supporting the niches are the sculptured camels of the three Wise Men.

Unfortunately, the stone of the exterior is so

friable that much of the fine old carving has perished. Within, the building is admirably decorated with bosses, each boss being different, and traces here and there of the original gilding heighten the effect. In the centre is shown the Star of Bethlehem, the holy emblem serving to connect the Nativity with the dedication of the chapel.

From the roof hangs a brass candelabra, which is engraved with the Nuremberg wings, and bears an inscription stating that it was presented by "Sir John Duddestone, baronett, 1696."

III

ST NICHOLAS' ALMSHOUSES

In St Nicholas' Almshouses, which I afterwards inspected, I could find nothing particularly worthy of notice except a large upper room called the belfry room. The curious old plaster ceiling holds quaint medallions of Matthew, Mark, Luke, and John with their emblems, which are represented in a very primitive fashion.

IV

COLSTON'S ALMSHOUSES

COLSTON'S Almshouses were founded by Edward
Colston in 1691. They have a large well-kept chapel,
in which pews, panelling, etc., of fine dark oak are
said to be of ship's timber.

The charity is administered by the Merchant
Seamen's Guild.

Edward Colston is buried in All Saints' Church,
Corn Street. There is, or was, a pretty custom of
decorating his statue with a bunch of flowers every
Sunday.

On the background of the monument is engraved
a list of his public charities, of which the total
amounts to £70,000.

An inscription says : " This great and pious benefactor was known to have done many other excellent
charities, and what he did in secret is believed to be
not inferior to what he did in public."

V

ST BARTHOLOMEW'S HOSPITAL

At the bottom of Christmas Steps is an Early English porch, very ancient and arresting. It is the only relic of a religious and philanthropic institution founded by a society of merchants for poor seamen at Bristol in 1445.

Formerly known as
St. Peter's Hospital, Bristol.
Now the Office of the Board of Guardians

(F. Bromhead, Clifton)

VI

ST PETER'S HOSPITAL

I OUGHT to apologise for introducing you to St Peter's Hospital, Bristol, for though at one time a charitable institution, it has now been annexed by the Town Council as offices for the Board of Guardians. It stands in a quiet square next to St Peter's Church, and during its long and varied career it has fulfilled many purposes.

It was first, in the year 1500, a private dwelling, afterwards a sugar refinery, then a Royal mint, and not until 1608 did the city acquire it as a home for paupers.

The beauty of its exterior, which is a really unique specimen of old domestic architecture, and the magnificence of its gorgeous hall, have tempted me to quote for you Mr Heath's description.

He says : " It is a beautiful apartment. The plaster ceiling is constructed in square- and diamond-shaped compartments, filled in with floral and other devices, while the deep cornice has a running series of armorial shields supported by griffins. For centuries this was all covered with whitewash, but some twenty years ago the encrustation was removed and the ceiling emblazoned with heraldic and other colours, in supposed accordance with the original decoration. The elaborate mantelpiece . . . shows a curious blending of Late Gothic with Jacobean ornament. . . . The large brass fire-dogs and the grate are worthy of attention.''

GATEWAY OF ST. PATRICK'S CHAPEL
GLASTONBURY

ST PATRICK'S AND ST MARY MAGDALENE'S ALMSHOUSES, GLASTONBURY

I APPROACHED Glastonbury for the first time in the golden ripeness of an August afternoon.   The marshy moorland and the meadows profusely set with apple trees lay in a haze, basking in the beauty of the sun- shine.   The old town was invisible, hidden in the folds of low hills, above which St Michael's Tor on my left and Weary-All Hill on my right rose pre- eminently.

Seen through that misty veil, with my thoughts perhaps somewhat attuned to higher visions by what I had read and heard, it seemed to me that Glaston- bury was suffused that afternoon with the radiance of a light that never was on land or sea.

Its origin takes one back into a dim past of whose centuries we can catch but a glimmer.   British Christianity claims the place as its cradle.   Irish Christianity has a hold on it through St Patrick, who was probably born there.   It is the well-spring of some of Tennyson's finest poetry.   Its mere name breathes mystic echoes.   Even the stirring deeds of early English history have not passed it by.

Small wonder, then, that to this day the town is

a point of pilgrimage for countless numbers, and that travellers from many nations crowd to its yearly summer festival.

We are told that at one time the district was broken into islands. Now the river Brue embroiders it like a silver thread, liquid record of bygone times, when it is believed the sea held sway there and Glastonbury went by the Celtic name of Ynysvitrin —the Glassy Island.

There in those distant days the scene was laid for great happenings. About sixty years after Christ, came from the south of France Joseph of Arimathea. Previously he had drifted—or so the French believe —with a band of followers, in a rudderless boat to the little town of Les Saintes Maries de la Mer at the mouth of the Rhone on the Mediterranean Sea. Even now at the end of July the day of their landing is celebrated there by a grand service and procession —one of the most picturesque ceremonies, by the bye, it has ever been my good fortune to see.

With eleven disciples, then, Joseph came to preach the gospel in Britain, bringing with him the Holy Chalice from the Last Supper. He moored his boat at the foot of Wyrral Hill—since corrupted into Weary-All Hill—and, ascending it, drove his staff into the rich soil as proof that the goal of his journey was reached. It is said that from the staff sprang up the Holy Thorn. The ancient tree itself is, of course, long since dead, but offshoots were taken from it, and three gnarled and venerable thorns which blossom twice yearly, at Christmas and at Easter, still exist in the town of Glastonbury.

Moreover, on the green slopes of Weary-All Hill may to this day be found a time-worn stone slab. It is graven, wonder of wonders, with J. A., the initials of Joseph of Arimathea. Tradition declares this marks the very spot where grew the Holy Thorn.

I am reminded by this legend of a similar one which obtains at San Francesco in Deserto, a small island near Venice. Here, one is told, St Francis once landed, planting his rod in the sand as he did so. The pious Venetians like to think that a large and hoary umbrella-pine at once began to grow on the spot. At any rate, there it now stands for all the world to see.

In Glastonbury, Joseph and his followers lived as anchorites at the foot of St Michael's Tor, and buried the Holy Chalice under Chalice Hill at its base. A perennial spring is said to have gushed from it, and to this day there are people who pin their faith to the curative properties of a draught of water from Chalice Well.

The tower standing on St Michael's Tor is all that remains of a church which St Patrick found there in ruins in the fifth century. He built another on the same spot, but an earthquake shock destroyed this in 1275. It seems to me characteristic of the wonderful happenings at Glastonbury that the old tower should have survived an upheaval which demolished the church of later construction.

As to Joseph, his most momentous action, and the one that had the weightiest result, was the making by him and his followers of a small wattle church, for which they used only the local reeds, soil, and stone. This, the Rev. L. S. Lewis, M.A., Vicar of Glastonbury, tells us, was the earliest known above-ground church in the world. Though the little place of worship perished long ago, the beautiful church of St Mary, sometimes called St Joseph's Chapel, was erected on its site. Even of that now only the shell survives, but in its ruin how glorious and impressive !

And now to turn to my quest, for, among the ancient remains of Glastonbury, my chief concern is with the houses of alms.

The most important foundation is sometimes called St Patrick's Almshouses, and is also known as the Royal Almshouses for Women, or Abbot Beere's Almshouses. He, by the bye, was the last but one of Glastonbury's abbots, and founded the alms-houses in 1512. They are tucked away in the rear of old buildings in the main street of the town, but the little chapel, dedicated to St Patrick, has first claim to our interest. It is within a stone's throw of the beautiful ruins of St Joseph's Chapel, and a small, low-arched doorway close to the almshouses, with a bell-tower on the top, leads into the shady precincts of the Abbey itself.

The Rev. L. S. Lewis tells us that St Patrick's, " built by the monks for their alms-folk, was spared

at the Reformation, when its lofty sisters were spoiled,
and all but demolished." The chapel possesses a
very ancient stone altar with a recess in its side,
likely to have been used for containing the priests'
vestments. Five crosses can be seen on the slab,
like those to be met with on the altar at Browne's
Hospital, Stamford. Outside the chapel door on the
right is a holy-water stoup, similar to the one at the
little chapel of St Margaret's, Wimborne. On the
exterior of the west wall are twin roses, a cross, and
two jugs. These are said by some to be a canting
rebus on Abbot Beere's name, but others declare
that they represent holy phials to contain the blood
of Christ.

One passes to the almshouses through an arched
gateway surmounted by a crumbling escutcheon, that
shows a Tudor rose and a cap encircled by a crown.
The heraldic beasts on either side are unrecognisable,
being much worn away. The dwellings now consist
of a neat row of comfortable modern cottages, built
to replace the old tenements, and the aged dames
seemed most happily housed there.

Leaving St Patrick's, I went in search of the almshouses for men, also built by Abbot Beere. From
Magdalene Street you turn down a narrow passage,
red-raddled and hard to find. Looking up, you see
the chapel belfry with a weather-beaten effigy said
to be the Magdalene in the bell-gable.

Two rows of low-pointed doorways give access
to the almshouses, formerly small cells occupied

by the monks. At one time each cell was boarded over half-way up, and thus divided into a dwelling with two rooms, one above another. About twenty-five years ago, however, the boarding was removed,

Belfry.
St. Mary Magdalene.
Glastonbury.

so that the cells are nearly twice as lofty as they were. Each occupant now has two adjoining rooms, every alternate door having been bricked up. Originally the alms-folk were eleven in number, but at present only five old men and their wives are accommodated.

The busy dame who took me round was highly

pleased with her apartments, and considered them most convenient, but to my mind the whole place sadly lacked light and air.

While we were chatting her husband came in. They told me he was eighty, and had been a traveller for a jeweller's firm. " I was a watchmaker too, and in a good position," he added.

Indeed, the little place was eloquent of his former calling, for clocks and watches were hung in every nook and corner. The walls were enriched with them, the shelves showed a goodly collection, and many ticked away in syncopated chorus. The room was crowded with furniture, ornaments, and pictures, and there was hardly space to turn among all the odds and ends.

" Just now," the old lady informed me, " only two of my five men have wives, so three of them have to ' do ' for themselves, and very well they manage it. One of them sews much better than I can," she declared ; " but I lend them a hand with the cooking at times."

I remarked to the old man, " A kind woman you've got for a wife."

To this he assented eagerly, " Aye, that she is ! She's a pearl. I shouldn't like to be without her."

His better half, much gratified, now fetched a key and took me into the chapel. It had a good arched ceiling, believed to be of oak, but the wood is hidden, more is the pity, behind a wash of pale blue. The oak beams of the walls, too, are partly plastered over with whitewash.   Round the cornice the Tudor rose, once gilded, appears at intervals, forming a .pleasing ornament between ceiling and wall.   The ancient piscina is still to be seen.

My guide pointed out to me with great pride a generous plot of garden available for each tenant. These green spaces must certainly do much to console the men for their restricted quarters.

It was pleasant to pass out of the narrow passage of the almshouses to the summit of Magdalene Street. There the town of Glastonbury ends somewhat suddenly, and a view across open country stretches before one.

Grassy meadows chequered with tiny canals, their banks fringed with pollard willows, spread away into the opalescent distance.   Fields of maize and apple orchards suggest the labour of the country-folk, who at evening trudge homeward along the shining ribbon of the roadway after their day's toil.

Standing there at the edge of the town and gazing first towards the old ruins and then across the wide space of country at my feet, I recognised something of the interest and beauty that must cling to this hallowed corner of God's earth as long as stone remains upon stone and those wonderful arches live, recalling in their graceful symmetry the past harmonious perfection of the whole.

It is, moreover, a land of romance that lies in its peaceful serenity before us.   Here Tennyson has

placed the final scene of Arthur's Passing, for this
is the Vale of Avalon :

> " Where falls not hail, or rain, or any snow,
>   Nor ever winds blow loudly, but it lies
>   Deep-meadowed, happy, fair with orchard lawns
>   And bowery hollows, crowned with summer sea."

The Passing of Arthur ! How long ago it happened we do not know, but we are told that the
bodies of the King and Queen found their final
resting-place, many centuries afterwards, by Royal
order, in a tomb before the high altar in the Abbey
church.

Could they look upon the Glastonbury that now is,
Arthur would surely say again :

> " The old order changeth, yielding place to new,
>   And God fulfils Himself in many ways."

HUGH SEXEY'S HOSPITAL, BRUTON

If you wander up hill and down dale through the fragrant valleys and over the wooded slopes of Somerset, you will come at long last to the little town of Bruton. It is set jauntily against rising ground, and below is stretched verdant pastureland threaded by the rippling waters of the Brue.

Here you will find an idyllic group of almshouses, owing their being to one, Hugh Sexey. Round this ample block of buildings Nature seems to have spread a spaciousness all her own, as if to fit the surroundings to the fine Elizabethan structure that crowns them.

Amplitude, a noble largesse, is not only Nature's keynote here, but the charity's also, for its endowment revels in the generous yearly sum of £4000, and nothing has been grudged to make of the place a worthy and even a luxurious home for the thirty old folk who are fortunate enough to find harbour there.

Sexey's Hospital stands flush with the road. Through a handsome gateway you enter into a courtyard, and the very first glimpse of it fills you with satisfaction, so absolutely right and harmonious

114

is its planning. On two sides of the quadrangle are rows of graceful arches. These support a wide balcony that is picturesquely enclosed by its Elizabethan palisade. The balcony affords a pleasant promenade for the old people, and an easy flight of steps gives egress to the courtyard. Beyond, through another gateway, you may gain the front of the Hospital, and here the view is charming and fills you with unstinted pleasure.

Large gardens slope downwards towards the river, crossed by alleys of velvet turf and shaded here and there by long pergolas roofed with roses, clematis, and other odorous delights. Between the grassy walks are wide flower-beds, and when I was there a perfect feast of colour enchanted me. Phlox, delphiniums, columbines, antirrhinums, hollyhocks, and other brilliant and upstanding blossoms of every hue were so tastefully grouped that they recalled, in modest miniature, the gay gardens fashioned for Marie Antoinette at Trianon by Lenôtre.

But at Bruton, in spite of all this beauty, utility has not been overlooked. Beyond the flower-garden and nearer the river are stretches filled with vegetables. Here and there twist the gnarled branches of venerable apple trees, and in August the old walls already showed a goodly promise of other fruit.

The courteous master soon presented himself and took me into the chapel. It is a peaceful old place. The ancient door by which we entered, as well as all the doors throughout the building, are still the original ones placed there. The panelling, oak pews, poppy-heads, and fine pulpit, skilfully carved and black with age, are a sheer delight. Here and there I found initials which had been cut by some lawless spirit in times gone by. I deciphered F. H. C., 1694 ; R. C., 1771 ; and another, 1714. It is supposed that this vandalism was perpetrated by venturesome schoolboys, for part of the building was formerly used as a school. After all, human nature does not change very much, though the centuries pass !

Upstairs the rooms with their old beams are most attractive. Their dimensions are generous—some of them I should judge to be at least fourteen by twenty feet. One of them—the board room—is panelled and carved in the Georgian style.

I was shown a marvellous old coffer with a most intricate piece of mechanism in the shape of a lock. Its springs and bolts are worked by the same key. This coffer formerly held the muniments, but the master, who, when I went over Sexey's, had only been installed a few months, had not been able to find the key, and so the contents had been removed. He opened the lid of another chest and showed me that it was filled to the brim with time-stained parchments and documents relating to the Trust. None of these he had, so far, found time to sift. Who knows what buried facts of interest may not come to light when all these papers are investigated ?

An old deed of George II has a curious casket, like a guitar-case and nearly as large. The ancient seal of the foundation is a very bulky object, as big and round as an orange.

We went into several other rooms, all possessing stout old beams. One of them is called the master's room, and is strangely divided by a wooden balustrade. Another had been used, I was told, as an infirmary.

Some of the rooms below have been ceded to the County Council, and in the old refectory the local Infant Welfare Centre meets weekly. Its members are enabled to attend mother-craft lectures in the adjacent dairy and roomy kitchen, and for a short time a girls' school was established at Sexey's Hospital. Later, however, this was discontinued. The refectory boasts a fine Gothic oak screen, but its table and an ancient "bread and cheese" cupboard have been transferred to the private rooms of the master.

I was then conducted to the basement and shown a stone well, dating from Elizabethan times. Its depth is at least forty to fifty feet. The water it holds is rich with iron, and the charming wife of the master told me she has applied it most curatively to many of the old folks' aching bones. How lucky they are to be watched over by such sympathetic and helpful people !

The kind couple took me into their private rooms and pressed me to have tea with them, and this, of course, I could not resist. The repast—for it was literally that—was laid in a lofty room with oak panelling and high Gothic windows, and well indeed did this beautiful setting suit its inmates. They seemed to radiate an atmosphere of kindness and goodwill, and they struck me as being most emphatically the right pegs in the right holes.

Under the master's ægis a good bath has been installed, and he pointed out to me with great pride a new invalid chair which had just been purchased.

" Is it really true," I asked, " that the founder of the Hospital, Hugh Sexey, was of very humble birth ? "

" Yes; he was the son of poor parents. They say he started life as a stable-boy at one of the inns in Bruton. But possibly he was ambitious. At any rate, he seems to have advanced from strength to strength. He actually achieved the important post of one of the seven auditors of the Exchequer, and kept this billet till he died in 1619."

I parted from my genial hosts with great regret. As I passed out into the courtyard, I noticed over one of the doors the bust of the founder with the inscription below it: " Laus Deo."

The dignified Elizabethan gentleman seemed to look down on his work with a benevolent eye. If he could return and see the admirable working of his charity, surely he might exclaim, " Behold, it is very good ! "

GREY'S ALMSHOUSES
TAUNTON

LEPER OR ST. MARGARET'S ALMSHOUSE
TAUNTON

GRAY'S HOSPITAL, TAUNTON

I HAD heard there were two, if not three, interesting almshouses to see at Taunton, wherefore one sunny August morning I set out in eager search of them. But no sooner had I left my hotel than I came upon a scene of surprising activity.

It was market-day. Women, intent on weekly shopping, hurried in from adjacent hamlets and from the outskirts of the town, pushing their babies in prams and go-carts in front of them. String bags, from which peeped out vegetables and paper parcels, were slung on the handles. Sturdy farmers' lads in gaiters drove sheep and young calves to the triangular market-place, which is the heart of Taunton. To it, like arteries, flow all its roads and byways.

Here a regular fair seemed to have sprung up overnight. Under huge white umbrellas vendors vaunted their commodities from brooms to braces. Stockings and sweetmeats vied with cheeses and framed oleographs for the favour of purchasers. Lawnmowers and lace—the cheaper Honiton variety —breeches, balls, baskets, and bee-hives competed for public patronage. Roundabouts revolved and swing-boats dipped and rose again, and above it all was the incessant tinkling of bells, the plaintive bleating of calves and sheep, and the anxious outcry of their mothers.

I picked my way down East Street through this herd of busy folk, and there, prosaically flanking the road for a hundred and thirty feet, I found, level with the pavement, the somewhat severe group of Gray's Almshouses.

They date from the seventeenth century, and have two arched doors. Over one I noticed the coat-of-arms of the Merchant Tailors' Company, and over the other the armorial bearings of Robert Gray, Esq., the founder.

The origin of this institution is recorded on a stone in front of the building as follows :

" Laus Deo. This charitable work is founded by Robert Graye of the Citie of London, esquier, borne in this towne, in the house adjoyning hereunto, who in his life-time doth erect it for tenn poore aged syngle women, and for their competent livelihood, and daylie prayers in the same, provided sufficient maintenance for the same, 1635."

In an old book by Joshua Toolmin, published in 1791, we see recorded that " Robert Graye left to the Merchant Taylors' Company for a dinner on the day of his funeral £40 ; to the parishioners £200 for a dinner for them and their wives; to his work-folks and wives—viz. the calendars and cottoners £60, and to his other workmen £13 6. 8."—so good cheer must somewhat have consoled them for their distress at losing him.

Wishing to explore the interior of the almshouses, I made my way through a narrow passage where an old man came to meet me. He was the " Reader," as the head brother is called here, and he takes the services daily, though not on Sundays. He told me that in olden times his office also entailed the teaching of reading and writing to ten poor children.

We first went into the oratory. It is a small room, but it is most completely furnished, and possesses the original old oak pews where the men and women sit apart, as well as a pulpit, all black with age. But the strange ceiling is the feature that most riveted my interest. It is decorated with a coloured design, showing a galaxy of suns and moons—or some such celestial orbs—overlying one another, so closely are they painted, and pierced here and there by long rays. It is sad to record that in one place damp from the room above has percolated—a great disaster, for the ceiling is certainly unique, and its colouring is so mellow that I fear restoration would be well-nigh impossible.

In the oratory there stands a large oak chest in which formerly the muniments were kept. It is built with a baffling lock and a tiny inner receptacle or coffer.

There is also a strongly painted portrait of the founder in black and scarlet robes with wide scarlet sleeves and a starched ruff. Here, too, another coat-

of-arms of the Merchant Taylors' Company adorns
the walls, with an inscription beginning D.O.M., and
notifying that this memorial in all humbleness is
erected to the Glory of God by the founder.

On the upper floor the women are housed. They
have each two rooms and a pantry, and the stairs
leading to their quarters are embellished with a massive balustrade.

On my way out I peeped into the garden at the
back, and was agreeably surprised by this view of the
buildings. Their picturesque gables and old roofs,
their quaint chimneys and an aged belfry, make quite
a pleasant picture, which I have tried to snap for
you. I was also much attracted by the two old
Tudor houses that adjoin Gray's. They belong to
the same charity and are dated 1638.

Next to these is to be found a block of buildings
called Pope's Almshouses. Their date is more
remote—1591—and their dimensions much more
humble than those of Gray's, but the old women
seem none the less thankful to be housed there.

I was now free to proceed to St Mary Magdalene's
Church, where, I had heard, is a life-sized figure of
Robert Gray that I had determined to see. As I
drew near I could not but admire the sumptuous
Gothic tower of the church. It is said to be a
faithful copy of the original that was removed in
1858, being unsafe.

Within, the nave has a well-preserved oak roof,
and in a recess in the north wall of the building

I duly came across the figure of Robert Gray, which looked down benignly upon me from its niche. Beneath is the following somewhat odd epitaph, that I have copied for you :

> " Taunton bore him, London bred him,
> Piety trained him, virtue led him,
> Earth enriched him, Heaven carest him,
> Taunton blest him, London blest him,
> This thankful town, that mindful city
> Share his piety and his pity.
> What he gave and how he gave it,
> Ask the Poor and you shall have it.
> Gentle Reader, Heaven may strike
> Thy tender heart to do the like.
> Now thine eyes have read the story,
> Give him the Praise and Heaven the Glory.
>   Anno Domini, 1635."

Strolling through the streets on my way home I recalled a few of the many historical associations that cling to the old town. The townsfolk of Taunton seem as proud of its story as if they, too, had weathered all the vicissitudes through which it has passed.

In 710, King Ina of Wessex pushed the invading Welsh back beyond the river Tone and fortified the place with a castle. Later, the Normans added their quota to the pile, and the mighty walls of their keep still survive. In 1497, that unprincipled and ambitious spirit, Perkin Warbeck, seized the town, but was unable to hold it. Here, too, in 1685, Monmouth was proclaimed King in the market-place. His glory, however, was short-lived, and after he was routed at Sedgemoor, Taunton came under the cruel sway of Colonel Kirke and Judge Jefferys, than whom no more tyrannical rulers have blackened the pages of English history. The Great Hall in the Castle is where Jefferys held his Bloody Assize, and visitors are still shown the place, outside the town, where Kirke penned those grim " lambs " of his. At the corner of the market-place and Fore Street, a shop now stands on the site of the house in which formerly the awesome colonel lodged. From the signboard here, we are told, he was wont to swing his victims in a most ruthless and brutal way.

It was a relief, after considering such horrors, to pass on to my next quest, the old Leper House of St Margaret's.

ST MARGARET'S HOSPITAL, TAUNTON

St Margaret's Hospital, East Reach, Taunton, also called the Leper Hospital, or Spittal, forms a small beauty-spot in an otherwise unattractive stretch of road. It can boast a very ancient foundation. In a history of the Hospital by the Rev. Thomas Hugo there is an allusion to an undated charter. This charter, judging by the names of the attesting witnesses, must have been made between 1174 and 1185, and therefore the even earlier existence of St Margaret's is suggested.

Later, the building needing repair and renovation, one regrets to read that three times recourse was had to the rather questionable method then in vogue of raising funds by the granting of indulgences.

A legend also tells us that misfortune overcame the place in the reign of Henry VIII, when tradition says it was burnt down. But if so, the sable cloud must have had its silver lining, for Hugo notes the rebuilding of the Spittal between 1510 and 1515 by Richard Beere, Abbot of Glas onbury, to whom we also owe the Royal Almshouses for Women in that ancient and wonderful place.

Of St Margaret's, Hugo adds that " the old

building seems to have escaped the general fate of
its fellows in the reign of Edward VI, and to have
been still employed in accordance with its original
use."

Those were days, however, of universal misrule.
Ignoring the welfare of humanity, men did what was
right in their own eyes, even if their actions injured
other people. Indeed, we learn from the following
memorandum in the Certificate of Chantries of the
time that, hard as it is to believe, part of the little
property of the inmates of St Margaret's had been
surrendered to the greed of the spoiler :

" Ther be wᵗ in the same Hospitall vj poor lazare
people, having for their relief . . . the same Hospitall, wᵗ a little orcharde adioynyng . . . wᵗ the
yerely Vs and also other small parcelles of lande . . .
and other relief they have none."

Nevertheless, one is glad to see that by some lucky
chance the little Spittal has weathered all storms.
It now consists of seven tenements ; but its income is
not large enough to support more than four pensioners, three tenants therefore pay a nominal rent.

The charity is available for women of good character, who have lived in the parish for a certain length
of time, and who, in the meanwhile, have not received
parish relief. They occupy two rooms, and are
entitled to medical attendance and four shillings
a week.

The Hospital once possessed a chapel, but all
traces of it, except a small portion of the outer wall,

have long since vanished. On the site, instead, is a cottage, which has greedily incorporated the only surviving fragment of the early chapel wall. The cottage is now used as a grocer's shop, and is covered with flaring yellow and red advertisements. I am compelled to own that they quite shock one's sense of fitness, and are a very unsightly appendage to picturesque St Margaret's.

The old almshouses, jutting out as they do at a blunt angle of a rather prosaic country road, form a delightful oasis in its somewhat tedious length. The quaint little block of thatched cottages, set in the flower-girt strip of garden, attracts the gaze of all. Every tourist hastening towards the town, whether in limousine or char-à-banc, cranes forward from the car to catch a fleeting glimpse of the Leper House.

Thin oaken pillars support the penthouse roof, which drops down to form a covered way in front of the tiny tenements. In the garden, a fragrant tangle of flowering shrubs has grown up, so that one only gets a hint of the mellow plaster and the low brick wall, on which are set pots of homely geraniums and mignonette. So deep are the shadows in that cloistered walk that one must draw very close before the ancient doors and windows can be discerned.

Inserted in the wall on the right is to be seen the Hospital's chief feature of interest. It is a boldly sculptured panel, placed there by the great Abbot Beere afore-mentioned, and displays his initials R. B., and above, a bishop's mitre, richly ornamented with gems. The carving is, alas, showing signs of the rough treatment and recurrent attentions of wind, rain, frost, and sun. But, at any rate, the main features of the panel survive to rejoice our twentieth-century eyes.

While I was admiring the treasure, one of the tenants appeared and beckoned me into her apartments at the extreme left of the building. Her living-room on the ground floor had a queer, old brick fireplace with hobs painted a shiny black. On the mantelshelf were two huge china dogs, brown and white, of the Cocker spaniel breed, and the walls were gay with the usual photographs and memory bits. Upstairs, her bedroom, with its cream colour-washed walls above and a neatly papered dado below, gave an impression of fresh cheerfulness.

" The wash did come off so on my clothes that I put up this paper myself," she said.

And when I congratulated her on the dexterity of her paper-hanging—

" Oh, yes," she answered, " I'm a very good paper-hanger. I've done a lot of that. It's wonderful what you can do if you try."

She then introduced me to another of the tenants, Mrs Thomas, a venerable and delightful dame, very nearly ninety years old, the show occupant of the almshouses. The other inmates had nicknamed her the Queen. She certainly was the merriest old soul, with shrewd black eyes which snapped with reminiscent enjoyment when she declared that she was the widow of a Crimean veteran, and had been a great traveller.

"Bless you, I'm an old warrior meself, I am," she said. "I've been with my old man all over England, Ireland, Scotland, York (!), and the Barbadoes. I keep them all alive here, I can tell you."

"I don't doubt it," I answered. "I can see that you are the life and soul of the place."

"That I am," she assured me; "they'd miss me if I was to go. And I enjoy meself, I can tell you. Why! I sing to them sometimes a bit. There was one song went:

" ' I've a husband of me own, his name is Willie Gray,
  And when I can afford it, the sov'reign I will pay.
  If you thought that I could marry you upon the first
      of May
  You must have been as green as water-creases ! '

Then I catch hold of me dress like this, and give them 'You should see me dance the polka,' " she quavered forth, suiting the action to the word.

"They want to know where I'm going to," she went on, "so I tell them I'll send them a post card. They say I can't do that from where I'm bound! So just to satisfy them, I mean to write the post card before I go! Then they'll be sure to get it ! "

Grim humour, this !

I have set down the wonderful old soul's words, but how reproduce for you her flashing eyes, the quivering eagerness in her face, the restless expressive gestures of her gnarled old hands !

Afterwards I asked her to pose for me.   She seemed highly delighted, and donned a clean white apron in honour of the occasion.

From the flagged pathway she waved good-bye to me as I turned to go homewards. The memory of her spare figure, of those snapping black eyes of hers, of the sunlight gleaming on her white hair, lingers with me yet.

PENROSE ALMSHOUSES
BARNSTAPLE

QUADRANGLE, PENROSE ALMSHOUSES
BARNSTAPLE

PENROSE ALMSHOUSES, BARNSTAPLE

THE gay borough of Barnstaple—a cheery old town
of whose wooded slopes the green margins are washed
by the flowing tidal waters of the river Taw—
though so far from London, the hub of England,
seems yet, in many ways, a very up-to-date centre.

Standing on its venerable bridge, which boasts
sixteen arches, and looking down stream, one notices
how the ancient town hugs the right shore. On the
left is marshy and sylvan country, and, right ahead,
the shimmering sea. When the tide is out, great
patches of sand—golden ochre in that silvery light
—form islets, the resting-place of countless gulls.
They stand huddled together in sociable contem-
plation, preening themselves and waiting the turn
of events, when the incoming tide woos them to
wider waters.

Looking up stream, however, the scene is quite
different. Barnstaple ends almost abruptly. Wood
and copse sweep down in luxuriance, and the Taw
is lost in fold upon fold of verdant growth. Standing
there, even in summer, you must wrap your scarf
closer round you and turn up the collar of your coat,
for almost at all times the wind blows so freshly with

the tang of the sea in it, that visions of Devonshire apples, cider, and clotted cream are not to be
postponed.

The town is rich in relics of the past. It has
several interesting old churches. To one of them,
St Peter's, a leaden steeple was added in 1388. It
seemed to me to lean at an angle almost as acute
as Pisa's tower.

Besides the Guildhall, which possesses many fine
portraits by Joshua Reynolds, there is the old
Grammar School, where the poet Gay, who was born
at Barnstaple, was educated. Then there is Queen
Anne's Walk, a beautiful colonnaded loggia with
a characteristic statue of the queen surmounting
it. In front is a round table, known in ancient times
as the Tome Stone. The Merchant Venturers, by
placing their purchase money on this stone in the
presence of witnesses, made the transaction a binding
one.

I was tempted to tarry among these survivals
of Barnstaple's past, but, remembering my goal, I
turned resolutely down Litchdon Street and soon
found the Penrose Almshouses. Here I happened
most opportunely upon the matron, a little rosy-
cheeked person, who smiled at me benignly from the
porch. She led me under an archway into a large
courtyard. An old wooden pump with a leaden
dome stands in the middle, and the twenty little
houses enclose it on all sides. The tenements are
occupied by forty people—seven men and thirty-three

women.   Two tenants, who call themselves partners, share a couple of rooms, and the rights of each are carefully guarded, even to the grates, which are divided down the middle with an oven on either side. From one, by the way, arose an insistent odour of onions.   The matron assured me that the division of the grates works exceedingly well.

" At any rate," she said, " one old lady cannot accuse the other of extravagance in the matter of coal ! "

This, of course, does not apply to the few married couples who share each other's worldly goods.

The almshouses have been furnished with an excellent laundry, as well as a wringer, etc., for the use of the occupants—a prosaic but much-desired boon.

All the doorways and the corners of the quadrangle were gay with bright flowers, and over the dripstones of the windows I noticed the initials J. P. of the founder, John Penrose.

Passing under another archway we came to a garden divided into twenty plots and planted with vegetables and flowers.   Those old women who are unable to cultivate their patches, lease them to outsiders and divide the money thus earned, while, in the case of the married couples, the husband undertakes this task and is able to sell his vege-tables.

We now returned to the arcaded walk with its squat granite pillars.   Chained to one of these is a time-worn alms-box. In the centre, over an arched doorway, I read the inscription :

> THIS HOUSE WAS FOUN
> DED BY MR. JOHN PENROSE
> MARCHANT, SOMETIME MA
> JOR OF THIS TOWNE ANO DN
> 1627.

These pillars support the penthouse roof, that is bordered with a delightful tracery in lead, most delicate and in admirable preservation. The design, a wild rose and its leaves, symbolises the founder's name, and roses occur again on the old doors, where they embellish the iron handles that work the latches. One door has a wicket, or hatch, of which the matron is immensely proud. She also drew my attention to the leaden-patterned framework of the windows, which are, moreover, filled with much of the original glass.

" Will you believe it though, ma'am," she added, " that many of the tenants say they like this clear modern glass best ! See, we have had to use it here, and here again, to replace broken panes."

On the right of the covered way is the chapel, which we now entered. It is remarkable for its beautifully grained oak. To a clamp of this had been linked an old Bible, which had somehow disappeared and whose loss my enthusiastic guide deeply deplored. I was allowed to turn over the leaves of a Prayer Book, dated 1745. I found in it a prayer of thanksgiving for the deliverance of James I from the Gunpowder Plot.

The matron evidently cherished every bit of the panelled old place, even to the pew seats, whose worm-eaten condition does not seem to give her a qualm. Framed on the walls of the chapel hang the rules of the institution. I was interested by one imposing the fine of 1d. on any absentee from morning or evening prayers, unless he or she be incapacitated by sickness or other cause. This wealth is divided amongst the rest of the old people.

Though now a place of "ancient peace," the Penrose Almshouses must once have seen a fierce conflict, for in the Barnstaple Records we read that—

" The 1st July 1644, a day never to be forgotten by the inhabitants of Barnstaple for God's mercie and favour shewed in that miraculous deliverance of them from that bloody conspiracy of some of our neighbours in inviting and bringing five or six hundred horse and foot, being French, Irish and some English against the town, with purpose to put all therein to the sword and to have possession them-selves of the whole town."

A recent note in the same record adds : " The fighting took place on Litchden Green, and there is little doubt that the bullet-holes in the oaken door at the Litchden (Penrose) Almshouses were made in the course of the attack."

Through that same door, with its bullet-ridden surface bearing grim proof of the foregoing, I now followed the matron into the board room. There hang two interesting portraits, one of John Penrose, a correct Elizabethan gentleman in pointed beard and ruff, by Cornelius Jansen, a Flemish painter who has evidently achieved an excellent likeness of his sitter. The other represents Mr Gilbert Paige, in Georgian dress, who, in 1835, founded the Salem Almshouses near by.

The old sundial over the arched doorway at length informed me of the unpleasant fact that time was flying. So I placed my offering in the alms-box and bade farewell to the matron, who told me wistfully that she had shown me all there was to be seen.

GREENWAY'S ALMSHOUSES, TIVERTON

In past days the old town of Twy-ford-tun, or Tiverton, as we now call it, was one of the busiest centres in England for wool manufacturing. But the recent tide of industrialism seems to have swept by, leaving the old place musing happily over former activities and but faintly stirred by modern commercial aims.

On high ground near the wooded Exe—and we all know how beautiful the Exe is—between the fertile fields of Loman and Exe River, then, the town stands, content to rest on laurels gathered for it by its doughty and adventurous sons of former times.

One of the most illustrious of these was John Greenway, born about 1460. He was of humble origin—a weaver—but his perseverance acquired for him abundance of this world's goods, and benevolent wisdom taught him how best to dispose of his wealth.

I have read a picturesque legend about him which runs as follows :

" Three times he dreamed, and thrice a mysterious voice bade him journey to London Bridge, where a stranger on a white horse would tell him some good

137

news. He accordingly visited the metropolis a little while after, and stood gazing on old Father Thames from the bridge mentioned in his dreams. Here he was accosted by the friendly horseman, who told him to go back with all speed to Tiverton and to dig beneath a certain tree. John, of course, did not linger on his homeward journey, and at the place indicated found a crock containing sufficient treasure to justify him in resigning his labours at the loom."

Like many of the great company of the Staple, John Greenway was one of the Merchant Venturers, or Seamen. To explain to you how the almshouses under his name came to be founded, let me transcribe the portion of his will bearing upon them :

" I, John Greenwaye of Tiverton in the County of Devon Merchaunte have ordained established builded and founded an Almshouse in the Burrough of the town of Tyverton aforesaid forever there contayned for the habitation of five poor men to have there continuall abideing and habitation in the same, and every one of them to have weekly every week in the yere and yerely and weekly for ever eightpence of good and lawfull money of England, to pray dayley for me the said John Greenwaye, Johannan my wiffe, and for all Christian people. . . . And the said eightpence I will that it be weeklye paid to everyone of the said poor men by the hand of such person or persons as hereafter in this my present will shall be nominated and appointed."

The generous plan was carried through, and in

1517 the building was erected in Gold Street. At first it consisted of two floors composed of six rooms to contain five poor needy inmates. It is in the Tudor style, and the chapel at the west end stands as originally constructed.

It seems marvellous that any part of the erection remains, for it has suffered during its long life three different fires. I simply must quote for you a contemporary account, by one Arthur Fisher, of the first of the conflagrations in 1612 :

" WOFULL NEWES

" from the West-parts of England.

" Being the lamentable Burning of the Towne of Teuerton, in Devonshire. Vpon the 5th of August last, 1612.

" . . . I must give you likewise to understand, of the wonderful preseruation of a School house (by the hand of God) with certaine almshouses which was a most rare and strange thing so hapning, and declares the great power of the Maker of heaven and earth ; for in the fiercest time of this consuming tempest when fire in the greatest fury flamed, invironing these silly cottages on every side, when helpe was supposed to be quite past, when other houses stood round about burning, they had no hurt at all, no, not so much as scorched, therefore wee may now say, it is the Lord that setteth up and pulleth downe, as himselfe pleaseth."

In the succeeding fires the almshouses, alas, did not escape scot-free, and in 1732 they were practically rebuilt. At this period, two figures which were saved from the fire, one of St Peter holding the keys of Heaven, with the motto, " O, St Peter, pray for us," and the other of St Paul, were once again embodied in the wall.

As the dwellings now stand they possess a square porch of great interest, as well as some inscriptions and a finely designed stone frieze—the latter has considerable artistic merit.

On the porch is to be seen the Staple mark of John Greenway, also two heraldic emblems, one showing the Royal arms of England and France encircled by the Garter, and the other the arms of the Courtenay family. Near these, the carving of an eagle holding in its talons a bundle of sticks recurs twice. This device has given antiquarians furiously to think, and has not yet been satisfactorily explained. We are told it is generally to be found in company with the Courtenay escutcheon.

The chief characteristic of these almshouses— and one, by the bye, that we are not allowed an opportunity of overlooking—is the very frequent appeal to the public for its prayers in favour of the founder.

Under the cornice I read :

> " Have grace ye men and ever pray
> For the sowle of John and Jone Greenway."

PARISH CHURCH
TIVERTON

WYNARD'S ALMSHOUSES
EXETER

On the side of the wall is alsc to be seen, under a Gothic niche, " Pr. for John and Jone Gr."

One is led to fear that the benevolent donor must have had many a misgiving as to his future state, for here as well as in St Peter's—the parish church of Tiverton, where both he and his wife are buried— he would seem to have lost no opportunity of repeating such entreaties, and his cypher and Staple mark as well. It was suggested to me that when founders of almshouses pray for their souls to be blessed and for residents and visitors to intercede for them, such petitions partake somewhat of the nature of a fire insurance policy.

On the pavement of the beautiful Greenway Chapel in St Peter's Church, then—it is a magnificent Gothic structure and quite dominates Tiverton—I duly found the brasses of John and Joan Greenway. He is shown in a long fur-lined gown with full sleeves, and a gypcière, or penner, and inkhorn are slung from his girdle. His hands are raised in prayer, while his feet rest on a little patch of flowers. He is bare-headed, with hair worn straight and long. Joan Greenway is seen in a high-peaked and embroidered head-dress. Her gown has tight sleeves and deep fur cuffs, and on her fingers are a wedding-ring and two other rings. A rich belt girdles her waist, fastened with three jewelled ornaments, and from them hangs a chain with a pomander and jewel; her hands also are lifted in an attitude of devotion.

The whole of this charming chapel, and the south

porch as well, were erected by John Greenway.　Both are most elaborately carved with representations of ships afloat on a wavy sea, wool-packs, horses, etc. The design was no doubt intended to record the fact that the founder belonged to the Guild of the Merchant Seamen or Venturers.　Running round the chapel on the corbel line are twenty scenes, done in relief, from the life of Christ, beginning with the Flight into Egypt.

Within the porch is an Adoration of the Virgin, and here again John and Joan are to be seen, kneeling on either side.

This church also holds the fine tombs of the founders of the Waldron and Slee Almshouses.　I now went in search of the first of these institutions.

WALDRON'S ALMSHOUSES, TIVERTON

I RECOGNISED the building at once by its square porch, so akin to that of Greenway's as to hint the probability that both were fashioned by the same hand, although the date of Greenway's is a few years prior to that of Waldron's.

The latter has a plain wooden gallery extending the whole length of the habitations, and between the four doorways, under this gallery, runs the inscription :

> " Depart thy goods whyl thou hast tyme,
> After they deathe, they are not thyne.
>> God save Queen Elizabeth."

The almshouses were founded by John Waldron, a native of Tiverton, born about 1520. He, like Greenway, was a prosperous merchant, but unfortunately he made no provision for the repair of the building, which therefore looks to its wealthier brother in Gold Street to help it.

On the cornice of the porch I made out the following quatrains in old English characters :

> " John Waldron and Richord his wife
> Builded this house in the tyme of their life,
> At such tyme as the walls wer fourtyne foote hye,
> He departed this world even the eyghtynth of July (1579)·

> Since youth and lyfe doth pass awaye
> And deathe at hand to end our dayes
> Let us so do, that men may saye,
> We spent our goods, God for to prays."

The chapel is insignificant and not very interesting. A very massive dripstone over the porch holds a shield on which, as at Greenway's, are combined the English and French arms.

The building is composed of eight small rooms for an equal number of poor men.   It has a tiny garden attached, and here still stands an aged yew tree, that is said to have existed as long as the building. This may well be, for nothing but an old trunk remains to tell the lingering tale of its life.

.   .   .   .

The third almshouse in Tiverton erected by George Slee, and formerly called the Great House of St George, or the Widows' Almshouse, is no longer in being, as far as the charity is concerned.   It was pointed out to me, and is a fine old house, but in a very dilapidated state.   " Nor," to quote a local authority, " is there any means existing by which it can be repaired."

WYNARD'S HOSPITAL, EXETER

NEARLY five hundred years ago a wealthy citizen of Exeter, a recorder of the city named William Wynard, read in his Bible the following words : " Go thy way, sell whatsoever thou hast and give to the poor."

He interpreted this command as addressed to himself and disposed of all his property, and in the year 1436 he built twelve houses for twelve poor men, each to receive two shillings a week, another house for a chaplain, and a beautiful chapel, which was dedicated to the Holy Trinity. Here services were held twice daily.

Not satisfied with merely erecting and endowing the Hospital, Wynard, like St Francis of Assisi before him, set the example of noble poverty himself. He took up his residence in his own almshouses, and lived and died among the other poor men who dwelt there.

His daughter Joan married Sir John Speke, and on the death of Wynard, Sir John became the patron of the Hospital in his father-in-law's stead.

But troublous times were ahead for Exeter. The city was invaded in 1643 by Cromwell, and great havoc was wrought, parts of the almshouses being demolished.

It was during these sad days that George Speke inherited the lands, and he, as an adherent of the Protector, not only refused to rebuild the premises, but also retained the money of the poor people. Later, it is true, justice prevailed, and the mayor and bailiffs exhibited a Bill of Chancery against Speke, so that in a few years' time the chapel and houses were restored and the foundation would appear to have been reorganised. The mayor and aldermen of Exeter were now appointed to visit the Hospital twice yearly, at Easter and Michaelmas, and Speke very rightly had to pay £100 damages.

In Magdalen Street, Exeter, this beautiful group of buildings still stands. Through an archway I penetrated into the cobbled courtyard, guarded on four sides by its friendly little houses of dark red stone. In the quadrangle is an ancient well, and keeping watch and ward over it a very aged tree. Both are railed off, for the fabric of the well is so old as to be dangerous—or so I was told.

I unearthed the matron, who had only recently attained to this post, and who apologised for her consequent shortcomings as a guide. She unlocked the chapel for me and, handing me a card recording some of the features of its history, left me to my own devices.

The small house of prayer is quite beautiful in a rich and sumptuous way. It has an early and finely carved stone gallery for the choristers, as well as some admirable old oak stalls, and the pews exhibit the usual poppy-heads. The high roof is arched and timbered, and at the cross-beams are to be seen delightfully worked bosses. The gorgeous effect of the whole place is due in a measure to the brilliant hues of the stained glass in the windows. Though modern and of no great worth, its presence is excusable because of the pleasant result.

At one time or another the chapel has been added to, a fine arch surmounted by a decoratively wrought stone cornice having been placed at the entrance to the chancel.

On the left is a brightly tinted monument. It completes the tomb of William Kennaway, who bought the patronage of the Hospital from Lord Frederick North, to whom it passed from the Spekes. The family of Kennaway are still the patrons of the chapel, and a good modern brass to one of the later descendants is dated 1887.

On the right wall hangs an antique wrought-iron stand, also brightly painted in gold, red, and blue, and surmounted by a crown. Its purpose intrigued me, for I could not imagine to what use it could be put in such a place. But I learnt later that it serves to hold the swords and maces of the mace-bearers who, fully robed, accompany the mayor when he attends service at the Hospital twice yearly.

On leaving the chapel I was invited into the apartment of one of the old men, who told me that he had just celebrated his golden wedding. His room is a very quaint one, with a tiny window in the fireplace over the grate. This is adorned with charming antique leaden tracery in a delicate pattern.

The old fellow was most contented with his surroundings, and spoke very gratefully of the present patroness, who supplements the grant of seven shillings by another two shillings a week.

"There's some that grumbles," he informed me, "and says, what's two shillings? But I says it makes nine shillings, and that's two shillings more than seven shillings, anyhow."

I bade farewell to him, and he kindly suggested my "giving a look" at the Livery Dole and St Anne's, two clusters of almshouses that it might be well for me to see.

The Livery Dole was founded on Heavitree Hill for the servants of an estate, and is so called from the enforced wearing of a livery by the old men who inhabited it. I was told several tales by the lively dame, Mrs Bright, who showed me round, and who remarked:

"Yes, ma'am, my name's Bright, and it's a bright day, and I'm bright by nature too!"

But her memory was not very bright, and I dare not take altogether as facts some of her picturesque anecdotes.

The names of the martyrs, Thomas Benet and Agnes Prest, recur to me in connection with the Livery Dole. For the sake of their religious convictions these victims were burnt at the stake in the years 1531 and 1557, near the spot where the almshouses stand. A monument now indicates the place.

From the Livery Dole I passed to a small batch of houses of alms at the top of Sidwell Street, which are grouped round a tiny chapel with an interesting history. The date of the original foundation of the religious house is unknown, but the present chapel was erected in 1418, and St Anne's Day, 26th July, has been observed here from time immemorial. In early days the place was a hermit's home, but it was later converted into almshouses for eight old people by the brothers Oliver and George Mainwaring. In the time of Cromwell it was used as a defence post, and was much injured by Fairfax's forces during the siege of the city.

The hermit's door is low and narrow—quite in the tradition—and I fancied I could still trace in the structure the cell that ages ago was inhabited by him. There are narrow oak beams in the vaulted ceiling, terminating in small carved heads, but unfortunately the wood is badly worm-eaten.

A most intelligent tenant took me into the old portion of the building to see her sitting-room, and pointed out the thickness of the walls, and the corner once occupied by a spiral staircase. And nothing would content her but that I must go upstairs into her bedroom to see the old beams that are secured by large pegs instead of nails.

" I du come up here and eat my bit of breakfast,"

she said, " for it seems more country-like seeing out " ; and, indeed, there were pleasant glimpses of green trees and distant hills between the modern roofs of the neighbourhood. " Yu wouldn't believe how I love my room and all these old things ! They be so interesting."

I had some difficulty to make her accept my usual little offering.

" I du love to show off the ancient things to folks who care. Oh, well, ma'am, thank yu very much," she added, as I bid her good-day.

JESUS' HOSPITAL, BRAY

THE leafy Berkshire country, undulating and beautifully wooded, had taught me to expect surprises at
every turn of the road. But I had never met almshouses as unusual and charming as those at Bray.

The beeches in their young tender green shone in
the warmth of the sunlight. Under the high blue
sky, dappled with golden clouds, the Thames flashed
silver and turquoise through emerald meadows
powdered with innumerable buttercups.

Everything wore a happy and radiant air; so
that, turning the corner of a village street and
coming face to face with the tasteful frontage of
Jesus' Hospital, Bray—mellow, brick-red, behind the
soaring pointed pyramids of its row of clipped yews,
with the sweeter amenities of purple iris, pansies,
poppies, and peonies in the sunny foreground—I
fairly caught my breath.

No one could fail to be justly proud of such a
delightful building. Perhaps that was why the life-
sized statue of the founder, William Goddard, arrayed
in doublet, hose, and ruff, seemed to smile down on
me with benevolent satisfaction from his niche over
the low arched doorway.

I went into the entrance porch and, ringing a bell, presented a letter which proved an open sesame to the kind chaplain's goodwill. He came forward and at once proposed starting a tour of inspection.

In the porter's lodge on the right hung a huge white-faced clock with clear black lettering.

" It seems rather to have taken the wall space for granted," I was moved to comment.

" You're right. It looks as if it had encroached. Do you know what it is ? It's one of the Act of Parliament clocks," said my guide. " They came into being in the time of William Pitt, you know. Watches and smaller clocks had had a greedy tax put upon them, that turned them into luxuries. It made them too expensive for the acquisition of many people. So these huge Act of Parliament clocks were put up in public places instead. This," he added, " is the original old alms-box. See, it has two locks. It is only cleared at Christmas-time with great pomp and ceremony."

We stood in the archway looking into the brilliant garden, of which the forty plots, one belonging to each resident, were bright in the sunlight. In the middle, near some clipped yew-hedges, stood a sun-dial.

" But what," I asked, " is that dark door with a shining cross on it at the end of the building ? "

" Ah, that," he said, " is the entrance to our chapel. The cross is on the altar, and it always shines out like that. You were admiring our gardens. Do you know that they suggested to the artist, Fred Walker, that beautiful painting of his, ' The Harbour of Refuge,' now in the Tate Gallery ? The members tend their plots themselves, or if they are not able to, a neighbour keeps them in order right through the year for the modest sum of twelve shillings. Sometimes even one of the other inmates takes on the job, and is allowed to pocket the proceeds. Now I want you to look at this old pump. The leaden panel with its raised devices is quite interesting."

He pointed to a lively cherub with puffed-out cheeks. At the four corners, the heads of lions, nicely modelled, were amusing, and obviously of the eighteenth century.

Within the chapel I noticed the delicate Jacobean screen, which is more daintily carved than most of its period.

Outside, my attention was drawn to the massive brick buttresses. The chaplain laughingly declared that they could have supported a majestic church three times the height of this little chapel.

" At first when I came here," he said, " I wondered why on earth they wanted to ' boost up ' a small building like this with such enormous buttresses. But an architect living in the neighbourhood explained to me that the soil about here is really only eight feet above the level of the river. If you dig down anywhere in these parts you come upon numberless springs. So no doubt it was the encroachment of the damp that they feared and were determined to guard against, even at the cost of so much brick and mortar."

We now followed a path and came upon several of the inmates who were working in their gardens. My guide introduced me to a fine old chap who was, he said, over eighty, and who was digging away lustily. Another old fellow, he told me, of about the same age, was nearly blind. He showed me his plot, where peas and onions were sown with almost mathematical precision.

" He does all this himself," said the chaplain.

" How is that possible, if he can't see ? " I asked.

" He keeps his lines straight by putting scraps of white paper on the mould. He can just see enough to be guided by the paper's whiteness."

Another veteran came out from a doorway of his potting-shed. With his square skull-cap and his gardening-apron, he put me in mind, for all the world, of one of the ancients in the *Meistersinger*.

Smooth lawns bordered by high poplars and flowering shrubs afford the happiest hunting-ground imaginable to these fortunate old people. Ancient oak pews, discarded from the chapel, are placed here and there about the grass. I spied a life-sized modelled figure of a man against a background of bushes with a springing hound at his side. He carries in both arms a large cornucopia. A hunting-horn hangs at his side, and he sports a tam-o'-shanter and a sporran.

" We can't make him out," said the chaplain. " The story attached to him, when he came into our possession, was of his being a doctor bent on entering a plague-stricken house. It was supposed that the dog tried to prevent this, but failed, with the result that the doctor took the infection and died. But then, why that cornucopia ? I'm afraid the mystery's insoluble."

I could not help saying, " He puts me in mind of the gallant figures of Scotsmen I remember as a child. They were to be seen standing with a debonair manner surveying humanity outside tobacconists' shops."

" Well, he came to us from St Peter's Almshouse, Wandsworth, when it was closed down. At first we were puzzled to know what to do with him. Then we tried him out here, and the surroundings seemed to suit him so well that here he has stayed ever since."

" He's lucky ! It's a lovely spot," I said.

" Yes, isn't it ? You can't think how the dear old souls enjoy themselves," said their kindly chaplain. " They play croquet. You should see how the old dames of over eighty relish their game ! And over in that corner I've had a swing placed. There's keen competition for that ! So there is for this summer-house. Look, I've had this shelf fixed with a hinge and they bring their tea out here. They like this little brook and the view over that meadow beyond. I've leased it for them."

" They're fortunate in their chaplain," I ventured to say as we walked back to the house together.

" Oh, I don't know about that.   Everybody's good to them.   Peep into this recreation hall.   We've a piano, you see, and all those books, and a platform behind those curtains.   The people in the neighbourhood are always getting up entertainments for our old folk."

He pointed to some commodious wooden armchairs.   " We want all the room we can get, I assure you," he added laughingly.   " Well, now I am afraid I must leave you.   Take as many photographs as you like while the sun's out, won't you ? and please don't hurry."

On my way back through the village I could not resist peeping into the church, renowned for its connection with the old song about the Vicar of Bray.

Here I discovered the fascinating monument to the founder of Jesus' Hospital.   The figures of William Goddard and his wife, Joyce Maunsell, delightfully quaint in their stone formality, face one another, and beneath are inscribed the following lines.   I quote them, as they seem a fitting ending to these notes on the founder's humane gift :

> " If what I was thou seekest to know
>   Theis lynes my character shal showe
>   Those benefitts that God me lent
>   With thanks I tooke and freely spent
>   I scorned what playnesse would not gett
>   And next to treason hated debt

I loved not those that stird vp strife
True to my freinde and to my wife
The latter here by me I have
We had one bed and have one grave
My honesty was such that I
When death came feard not to dye."

CHRIST'S HOSPITAL, ABINGDON

In the old town of Abingdon, one of the most paint-able of our river homes—its banks are washed by Father Thames, and its more renowned sister city, Oxford, lies but a pleasant reach of a few miles upstream—in this once famous little town, then, is to be found Christ's Hospital, an almshouse that is, perhaps, as picturesque as any we have yet visited.

It nestles—one of a knot of three such habitations, of which the other two are Twitty's and Brick Alley Almshouses—round the beautiful old church of St Helen's, forming thus a small centre of historical interest to the town.

Let us first explore the most outstanding of them, Christ's Hospital, for not only is its exterior irre-sistibly alluring, so that one is not proof against so much structural beauty, but also because its claims to our interest exceed those of its less romantic kindred near at hand.

It makes no pretensions. Indeed, if you catch sight of it first from the opposite bank of the river, your glance is merely arrested by the end tenement of a line of cloistered dwellings, protected from too

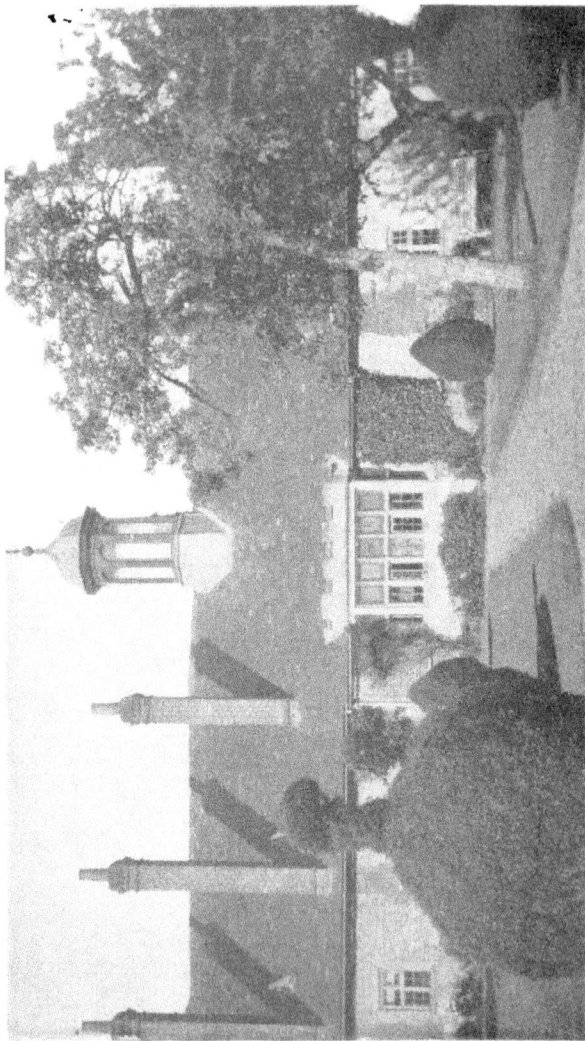

CHRIST'S HOSPITAL
ABINGDON

inquisitive prying by ancient iron railings and a small gate. But you have only to pass through, and what a different impression you at once receive! On the right, beside an asphalt path, is a long procession of majestic trees bordering the old graveyard, and polled in order, no doubt, to admit all possible sunshine.

On your left extends the cloistered gallery of the homely little almshouses with their comfortable sheltering roof. They have a tall lantern, and below it projects a porch, cosy in winter and, in the summer, providing shade. At the summit of the lantern a gilded vane veers gaily against the blue sky. The front shows a symmetrical row of arches that terminate in satisfying perspective at the end of the walk.

How deep and cool is the darkness between those arches! How orderly the ranged regularity of their gleaming pillars! As if to complete the picture, the sun has spread for our special behoof delicately traced shadows of the clipped tree-trunks across the silver-grey of the path.

Come with me through the porch and we will entice the house-proud matron to take us into the hall and point out to us its claims to attention.

First of all let us notice the Jacobean panelling, harmonising with the ancient flap-leaved table of oak. Both are a little anterior in period to the set of Chippendale chairs with which the room is furnished, but as these are also in oak and wonderfully fine, we cannot be so captious as to cavil at them. There is as well a six-legged table in the same wood dating from James I.

On the wall hangs a very quaint old picture known as " The Bridge Builders."　The rebuilding in stone, in 1416, of Abingdon's old wooden bridge must have supplied the artist with the subject for this painting.　In those days, it seems, bridge-building was a noble and holy mission in many European lands. Indeed, French tradition says, we may remember, that at Avignon the lad Bénézet was divinely in-spired to lay the foundation stone—a gigantic and abnormally heavy one—of the famous bridge there, and he was afterwards canonised as a reward for his great effort.

In the case of Abingdon, the work was carried out by the Brotherhood of the Holy Cross, who built the original almshouses in 1446.　They maintained a bridge priest, and the poem hanging on the wall in the hall explains the motive for the construction of the bridge.　It begins :

" Of all Werkys in this Worlde that ever were wrought,
　Holy Chirche is chefe. . . .
　Another blessed besines is brigges to make."

To my sophisticated eyes the primitive painting shows, I must confess, humorous features.　In the background of the picture the workmen are busy at their task.　In the foreground the masters are depicted with long shoes and gowns that must

certainly have hampered their movements.   Below
the picture is inscribed :

" In memory of Jefforye Barbvr and John Howchion,
Benefactors."

Now let us examine the old alms-box by the door,
and contribute our mite, for history tells us that
Samuel Pepys, when he came to Abingdon, did the
same.   You may here read the account of his visit
in 1668, when he stayed at the Antelope Inn—
now the very same Queen's Hotel where we are
housed.

" *July* 18*th*, *Wednesday.*—Up and walked to the
Hospitall.   Very large and fine and pictures of the
founders and the history of the Hospitall and it is said
to be worth £700 per annum, and that Mr Foley was
here lately to see how their lands were settled.   And
here in old English the story of the occasion of it,
and a rebus at the bottom.   So did give the poor,
which they would not take but in their box, two
shillings and sixpence.   So to the Inn and paid the
reckoning and what not.   Thirteen shillings.   So
forth towards Hungerford."

The old silver badges hanging on the walls of this
room are interesting.   They are not now worn by
the inmates, but in former times were used to adorn
their long blue gowns.

Here in the hall the fourteen residents assemble
for prayers, and the occupants of Twitty's and
Brick Alley Almshouses are also admitted to the

services. All denominations are received at Christ's Hospital, as there are no religious restrictions. This broad-minded principle has obtained ever since King Edward VI re-established the foundation as a purely secular charity.

The beautiful bay window with its charmingly designed leaded frame shows us various coats-of-arms, amongst them the blue lion of Sir John Mason who, with Edward VI, helped to refound the almshouses in 1553—a few years after the dissolution of the Guild of the Holy Cross. Admirable portraits of both the king and Sir John look down on us from the walls—the one of King Edward is a really good piece of work. And as we are now leaving the hall, and are once more in the gallery, let me just draw your attention to portraits of these same founders, as well as to some other pictures which, though rather faded, are to be seen on the exterior of the building.

Finally, let us go round to the beautiful garden at the back of the almshouses. Here are smooth lawns, wide gravel paths, beds of fragrant and old-fashioned flowers, and bushes cut into fantastic shapes. Here, too, we must notice again the octagonal lantern rising gracefully above a series of tall chimney-stacks, and we cannot help admiring anew, from the outside, the beautiful mullioned window of the hall with its embattled cornice.

As we tear ourselves regretfully away from the matron, she tells us that the garden has often been the resort of artists, who have perpetuated its peaceful charm.

.   .   .   .

In Ock Street, where are many old-fashioned dwellings, we will now glance at Tomkins' Alms-houses, a double row of cosy little cottages built and endowed by Benjamin Tomkins in 1731 for four men and four women.

Let us effect an entry for a few minutes with the milkman, who is going through the gate, and admire the cobbled pathway, embellished on either side with rows of cheerful flowers and flowering shrubs. At the far end, under the Georgian cupola and the inset inscription to the founder, is an archway. It leads to the tiny kitchen gardens allotted to each tenant, and on the left we can see the small staircase by which one climbs to the belfry.

The wife of one of the tenants tells us that she is paid five shillings a week for looking after the other old folk. There is, it appears, one aged man of nearly ninety whose sight is failing. Yet on fine days he sallies forth to work at some light job, and is thus able to eke out his pension. Tomkins' Alms-houses have a clean, pleasant, and cheerful aspect, and the old people here must be very comfortable.

THE HUNGERFORD ALMSHOUSES,
CORSHAM

The praises of the Hungerford Almshouses at Corsham had so often been sung to me, that I determined to take the first chance of visiting them, and a fine summer's day seemed to offer itself for this pleasant purpose.

Nearing the little town, I noticed much activity in the neighbourhood of several stone quarries, and on inquiry was told that Corsham yields most of the stone used in the production of what is known as Bath stone.

Many picturesque old buildings have gone towards the making of the place. The line of the High Street is pleasantly broken by the pointed gables of some quaint and venerable Flemish houses. I was also particularly attracted by the ancient inn, the Methuen Arms, near a stately avenue of trees leading to Corsham Court, the seat of Lord Methuen. This fine house was built in 1582 by William Halliday, Esq., whose daughter Margaret married Sir Edward Hungerford and founded the almshouses between the years 1668 and 1672. After belonging to various families, the property was

THE HUNGERFORD ALMSHOUSES
CORSHAM

BROWNE'S HOSPITAL OR BEDEHOUSE
STAMFORD

finally purchased in 1747 by Mr Paul Methuen, and, as we have seen, his descendants still own it.

This gentleman, by the bye, would seem to have been somewhat of a humorist. He never married, giving as his reason for bachelorhood the excuse that the blessing of wedlock was too great for him to enjoy ! No doubt privately he regarded it as a questionable one.

Corsham itself has a notable history leading back to a much earlier date than the foundation of Corsham Court. Tradition tells us that it was the occasional abode of kings, as we may read in the *Chronicles of Robert of Glo'ster*, where he speaks of "Kyng Ayldred" (Ethelred), who "lay syk in the town of Corsham." This was probably in A.D. 1011, when King Swein and his son Canute marched through Wiltshire and exacted heavy extortions from the people, and King Ethelred being ill at Corsham, his son, Edmund Ironside, took the field, attacked the invaders, and forced them to fly to their ships.

At any rate, Corsham was a Royal manor from the days of King John. It was bestowed upon Princess Mary, daughter of Edward I, but, much to her father's chagrin, she refused it and, instead, took the veil in Ambresbury Nunnery. Edward II gave it to his favourite, Piers Gaveston, and afterwards it formed part of the dowry of several queens. The town, indeed, had so many connections with Royalty that it gained the title of Corsham Regis. Leland, who visited it in the time of Henry VIII, writes of "Corsham, a good uplandish town, where be the ruines of an old manor place; and thereby a park wont to be yn dowage to the quenes of Englande."

Walking down the High Street, I came to the south end of the town and found the old almshouses. But at first it seemed difficult to believe that this stately building, with its beautiful oriel porch, its Gothic windows, its graceful bell-turret, and its row of aged pollard willows, could have been destined for so humble a purpose, especially when I further noticed over the porch the elaborately carved Hungerford arms. These are embellished with many sculptured emblems, amongst them the garb of the Peverils and the sickle of the Hungerfords. The whole façade seems more that of a rich old manorhouse than of a benevolent institution for housing six old women. The north and west fronts bear tablets to the memory of Lady Margaret Hungerford.

As I stood gazing at the building and pondering the beneficence of the founder, one of the tenants came out to me and I begged to be allowed to see her quarters. She led me through her sitting-room to quite a spacious bedroom above. It contained many cherished possessions, among them two fine Queen Anne chests-of-drawers, a beautiful satinwood bedstead, and a round Chippendale loo-table. On the floor were spread many gay patchwork mats, which she informed me were her own work.

"Is it possible that all the tenants have such fine bedrooms?" I inquired.

"I don't know, ma'am," came the prim answer;
"I don't go about in other people's houses."

Old Porch,
Hungerford
Almshouses,
Corsham.

The exclusive dame went on to say that she was
eighty-nine on her last birthday.   She certainly bore
her years bravely and was most erect and alert.

"You must see our cloister," she said, and conducted me to a long flagged passage at the back of the building. A sloping roof is supported by weather-beaten oak pillars, which are roughly carved here and there. Running the whole length of the cloister are little gardens, some of which were gay with flowers. Each is divided from its neighbouring patch by a low stone wall, and this ensures the privacy apparently so dear to some of the inmates.

" That door," said my guide with bated breath, pointing to a little doorway on the right, " leads to the warden's house, so that she can run in and see how we're getting on."

After admiring the flowers, I bade farewell to the old almswoman, and went to the main entrance in search of the lady who has unselfishly undertaken the duties of warden and who showed me the interior of the hall.

Entering it, one's first impression is that it must have been a chapel, for at one end is a small old pulpit. I was told, however, that the place had never been consecrated, but was used in former days as a school. The pulpit is of the two-decker type. The schoolmaster's seat and desk would have been above, and below, in the clerk's place, a folding bench was probably occupied by the usher or head scholar. Against the walls are set oak pews of which the back row is raised, and here the old women from the alms-houses were accommodated for morning and evening prayers, while the rosy-cheeked school urchins filled the front rows. The school is no longer in existence,

and the building has passed into the private owner-
ship of the warden.

The hall has been very artistically and cosily
arranged as a charming dwelling-room, and presents
a most alluring picture with its fur skins, its antique
Oriental rugs, its many books, and its family portraits
adorning the walls. In the corners, as well as on the
old hearth, stood tall vases of flowers and tastefully
grouped ferns.

At the other end of the room is an oak gallery,
richly carved and decorated with coats-of-arms. The
oak has evidently never suffered the vandalism of
varnish, but has been harmoniously mellowed by
that supreme artist, Time. Three lofty windows,
eighteenth-century additions, have greatly embellished the hall. Besides increasing the light, they
add a real sense of height. Except for these
windows, the place stands as it was originally
built.

About sixty years ago the old fireplace was opened
out and, during some later repairs, a fragment of
the former building material—a section of plaster
and reeds—was discovered by the warden, who said
that reeds of the same kind may still be found in
the neighbourhood to this day. She has quite a
collection of ancient relics acquired from time to time
on the spot. I wish I could recall for you her
enthusiasm as she handed me various objects,
treasured by her reverently. In a series of trays she
has arranged some ancient hand-made pins, a few

sulphur matches that, though made centuries ago, looked almost as if manufactured yesterday, various old glass bottles and an essence bottle, as well as coins of many dates.   One of these is a token-coin of James II, who, during his campaign in Ireland, lacking money to pay his troops, melted cannon, etc., of which the metal was made into tokens.   She had also found some clay pipes of the time of Charles II and James II, a parchment copy-book, and an old song book with the inscription, "T. Bishop, 1775," as well as a prescription on parchment for bleeding. A quaint apple-corer, fashioned from a deer-bone, took my fancy, and I was given to understand that the same kind of implement is used in the village to this day.

When at length I had examined all the treasure-trove, I felt I must have trespassed on the good nature of the kind warden.   As I took my leave I ventured to tell her how fortunate I thought it for the Hungerford Almshouses to have fallen into such appreciative hands.

HALL'S ALMSHOUSES, BRADFORD-ON-AVON

FROM Corsham I drove through pleasant leafy ways to Bradford-on-Avon, where, I had heard, was to be found an interesting little group of almshouses. The small town, contemplatively perched upon its hill-top, is centuries old. It rises in low terraces that are reared one above another. In the valley winds the silver Avon, and at Bradford it is spanned by an ancient bridge. Midway across it is to be seen a charming little cupolaed chantry, and of these bridge-chantries England can only boast three, Rotherham and Wakefield owning the other two.

With its piled-up dwellings, and at its feet the river passing beneath the bridge and chapel, Brad-ford's seemed to me a miniature English version of world-famed Avignon Bridge, where, in olden times, everyone was wont to dance. Luckier than its French relative, however, the Bradford Bridge is complete, whereas at Avignon only two-thirds remain.

The almshouses form a small oblong building approached from the high-road by a flight of steps. These are flanked on either side by a square ball-topped pedestal. A low wall encloses a terraced walk, and here the old men were sunning themselves. Between the two centre windows is a shield bearing the crest of the founder, John Hall—three battle-axes and the motto, " Deo et pauperibus." Hall founded and endowed the place in 1700. The almshouses are occupied by four poor men and their wives.

It was pleasant to see the old couples passing their last wedded days together, though one regrets that, when the husband dies, his widow is forced to find fresh quarters.

BROWNE'S HOSPITAL OR BEDEHOUSE, STAMFORD

I WENT to the old town of Stamford in Lincolnshire with interest already kindled, for the charms
of Browne's Hospital had often been described
to me.

I approached the place from the south, and could
not help noticing the changes in the landscape as
we bowled into Lincolnshire. The villages have a
character all their own. As I sped quickly along,
their mellow stone cottages, with tall chimneys and
thatched roofs, seemed part of the very ground
beneath them, and one was almost tempted to think
they had grown out of the soil, so closely do they
resemble it in the green-bronze of their complexion.
In the distance, indeed, it was only the glint of the
sun on a diamond-paned window, or the thin blue
spiral of smoke from some upstanding chimney, that
helped to distinguish the shyly nestling hamlets
from their surroundings.

The Lincolnshire fens lie still far away, and the
land I passed through is undulating and pastoral,
with fine groups of trees, massy hornbeams, sturdy
oaks, and towering beeches. Here and there, it is

true, one comes across meadows, flat and sedgy, where sleek cows feed or rest in their hundreds, but they seem equally contented on the higher land of open ridges. Lincolnshire throughout, though a hunting county, is a grazing agricultural county as well—the Eldorado of the cattle-breeder and well-to-do farmer.

After quitting a charming little village, Dudding-ton—a thatched uphill and down-dale village, all ochre and green—it was just before entering Stam-ford that I caught a tantalising glimpse of the gates of Burghley House, the Marquess of Exeter's stately home. It had been built originally, as everyone knows, by the great Lord Burghley, Lord High Treasurer of England in Elizabeth's reign. His descendants have dwelt there down to the present day. Amongst them was Henry, the tenth earl, and Sarah his wife, known as the Cottage Countess. Her maiden name was Hoggins, and for two or three years after their marriage, or so the tale goes, they lived in rustic retirement, calling themselves Jones. Tennyson, as you may remember, has immortalised them in his poem, *The Lord of Burleigh.*

Time and space, alas, forbid my taking you now to Burleigh House, though I should dearly like to show you the portraits of the romantic landscape painter and the " simple village maiden," whose courtship gave the great poet his theme. These pictures, as well as many glorious works of art by Velasquez, Rubens, Titian, Dürer, and a host of other artists

no less distinguished, hang in " Burleigh House by
Stamford Town."

Turning into St Martin's Road and dropping down
the hill, I soon reached my destination, the quaint
old George Inn.   Here, in 1634, Charles I and Queen
Henrietta Maria spent the night.

The ancient borough of Stamford is such a wonderful old place, and has been so mercifully as well as
artistically dealt with by the builder and restorer,
that one is luckily not forced to chronicle any
renovating barbarisms.   The harmonious features it
presents are to this day those of a mediæval town.
Where, here and there, rebuilding has been necessary,
the stone used, Barnack Rag, or Stamford stone, is
of such a nature that, in a year or two at most, it
has assimilated the soft bronze tones of more time-
worn buildings.

The old place is thronged with points of interest.
In every narrow street you come upon forgotten bits
of stone-carving, hoary oaken beams, and surviving
portions of arches, partly swallowed by more recent
houses that have encroached upon them.   It is, too,
a town of churches—at one time it possessed sixteen
—and many of them are so well placed in quiet cobble-
stoned closes, that we modern folk with our high-
heeled shoes and modish clothing, with our hooting
motors and ear-splitting motor-bikes, seem utterly
out of the picture.

But in the early part of the thirteenth century the
Stamford streets rang with quite a different clamour.

Burton, in his *Rambles Round Stamford*, tells us that, in the reign of King John, two bulls were fighting in a meadow. When a butcher parted them, one of them ran into the town and, infuriated by dogs, "it tossed all and sundry." But a noble Earl apparently enjoyed "the sport" [*sic*], for he gave the meadow to the butchers on condition that they provided a bull to run annually through Stamford on 13th November! This obstreperous pastime lasted through six centuries until, in 1839, it was at length put down.

I find it hard to resist leading you at once to St Leonard's Priory, a marvellous and historic old building, founded by Wilfrid in A.D. 665 for the Benedictine monks. Now it is used as a farm building, and is stacked high with corn and hay, and lumbered with trolleys, mowing-machines, and the like, so that one can only just descry the Norman and Gothic splendour of its arches and windows. Thus vanish the glories of the world, both spiritual and temporal!

In the garden of the town clerk's house at the top of Barn Hill is to be seen a fine arch under which Charles I passed on his flight from Oxford to Newark. At that time the house belonged to Alderman Wolph, and here the king lay for the night. Soon afterwards, however, as we know, he was captured, handed over to the Roundheads and executed. The Stamfordians, therefore, claim that he spent his last night as a free man in the old house on Barn Hill.

CEILING, CALLIS HOUSE ALMSHOUSES
STAMFORD

OLD WALL, BEDE HOUSE
HIGHAM FERRERS

Then there is the oaken door of Brasenose Girls' School, where once Brasenose College stood.   On this old door hung, in those early days, a famous and much-disputed knocker, placed there when a band of students, seceding from Oxford, established them-selves with their prize, the knocker, at Stamford. Here it remained for over five centuries, until about 1888, when it was repurchased by Brasenose College, Oxford.

A little farther along the same road, St Paul's Street, is one of the most ancient schools in England. Parts of it are remnants of a church of the early thirteenth century.   St Paul's Street and Broad Street, indeed all the old streets, abound with interest-ing bits, types of the domestic architecture of many periods.   Every little nook and cranny, every narrow passage or " lane," can boast its relic of bygone days. It would be delightful to explore them with you, but our business now is with Stamford's almshouses.

Before visiting the most outstanding of them, Browne's Bedehouse, come with me, for we may not have time afterwards, to a diminutive cluster of ancient dwellings for the poor which stand on the south side of St Peter's Street.   They were endowed by a local grocer, George Williamson, in the sixteenth century, and housed six poor widows.

In a compact and cosy room on the first floor, that may once have been the master's apartment, is to be seen a remarkable moulded ceiling.   The old lady whom I found living there was hugely proud of it,

12

and declared the subjects were drawn from the Apocalypse and from the story of Susannah and the Elders. She went so far as to hand me her Bible, that I " might read all about it."

Certainly the mouldings are admirably preserved, though the quaint humans, birds and beasts, depicted strike one as naïve—to say the least of them!

And now let us turn to the old Bedehouse, or Browne's Hospital, which was founded in the reign of Edward IV by William Browne, a merchant of the Staple. Leland tells us "he was a marchant of a very wonderful richnesse," and truly the group of buildings we owe to him still bears ample witness both to the wealth and to the generosity of the benevolent wool merchant. He died before the structure was completed, and his brother-in-law, Thomas Stokke, finished the good work.

Through the porch one gets a fascinating glimpse of the old cloisters and a sunlit corner of the garden they enclose. But I heroically resisted their appeal and rang the bell at the house of the warden, who had kindly undertaken to show me round—a privilege I deeply appreciated. Nothing, indeed, can surpass his keen enthusiasm and the wealth of lore that he has acquired about the old place, though it is less than two years that he has held the appointment.

He led me first into the lower hall, which was formerly the dormitory of the brothers. Its ceiling is finely beamed, and at one time it had five cubicles on each side with a broad passage between. They no longer exist, and the hall now serves instead as a grand council chamber. A splendid open screen of carved wood in pure Tudor style divides it from the little chapel. The warden told me that this beautiful screen has, alas, been attacked by the death-watch beetle, against which fierce war is being waged.

The chapel also possesses a fine old cope chair, and some skilfully carved pews with poppy-heads, and miserere seats of varying designs. Its stained-glass windows, besides, are greatly cherished treasures of the Hospital, for they have been put together with priceless bits of ancient glass saved from the original foundation. They show portions of many Biblical subjects, amongst others St John the Baptist, St Catherine with her Wheel, a Royal saint, probably King David, the Virgin Mary, the Holy Trinity with St Barbara, who holds a piece of architecture in her hand, and St James in palmer's attire, with a nameless female saint below, as well as Solomon and Seneca, standing for wisdom and philosophy. The jewelled crowns of these saints glow as brilliantly as though really set with gems.

Appearing constantly among the other subjects I noticed the crests of the Browne family. Two emblems of these crests refer to the occupation of wool-stapling. They show three hammer-like objects meant to represent the staples used to secure the wool, a row of teazles employed in the combing of it, Stokke's crest, a stork rising from its nest, and a heart enclosing the letter B.

A vastly interesting relic remaining in the chapel is the old altar-slab formed from Barnack Rag. It is eleven feet long by over three feet broad, and five crosses are engraved on it. The edges of the incisions are still sharp and unrubbed, and the warden said this supported the theory that during the Cromwellian Civil War the altar-slab was removed and placed, inverted, on the threshold of the chapel. This was done in order to conceal the holy purpose of the slab, otherwise it might never have survived the depredations of the Roundheads.

The warden then led me upstairs to the audit chamber, a spacious apartment over the hall. It also has a handsome ancient carved screen and some interesting massive furniture of the sixteenth and seventeenth centuries. On the table under a glass shade stands a very old alms-box, which was found buried in the eastern wall during the restoration of the fabric. Still lying within the box is some finely woven linen, yellow and stained with age, and untouched since the fifteenth century.

Right along the cornice I noticed a wire supported by hooks. The wire, however, seemed to have lost its purpose, for it ran along the frieze with nothing hanging from it.

" Ah, you're looking at that wire, I see," said the warden. " These walls used to be hung with antique tapestries, but, alas, they have vanished from our ken, nobody knows whither, and that denuded wire is all that is left of them. But now I'll show you something that has remained with us." He unlocked a cupboard and produced a venerable book.

" This is a Breeches Bible." He pointed to the passage in Genesis from which these rare volumes take their name, and in which Adam and Eve are described as making themselves breeches of fig-leaves instead of aprons. He also showed me a massive muniment chest. It is crammed with documents which the warden so far, owing to the short time that he has been at Browne's, has not been able to investigate. The great chest has huge iron bands and three locks, all different.

" I'll unlock it for you," he said, " so that you may see I can't show you more of it." He did so.

" That doesn't open it, you see, because of these two other locks, and they are padlocked. I'm not trusted with their keys ! Two of the trustees hold these, so that the chest can't be opened unless all three of us lend a hand. This is to prevent abuses. Formerly, the moneys of the foundation were kept here, and sometimes they were misappropriated or abstracted. So the trustees thought that by giving three of us separate keys they were safeguarding the contents. After all, it wasn't likely that all three of us would be thieves, even if one of us was ! "

The idea was doubly humorous because the huge chest, though its wood is worm-eaten here and there, looks as if it could resist the unlawful pillaging attempts of a whole army at least.

Descending again to the ground floor, I noticed an old inscription on brass let into the wall. Some say it is from the pen of Stokke, but others affirm that Browne himself may have been the author of it, as well as of some equally quaint verses to be found near his tomb in All Saints' Church, which we will visit later.

Let me transcribe for you those on the brass plate of the Bedehouse wall :

> " This structure now contains twelve habitations
> Which shall remain for future generations,
> For old and poore, for weak and men unhealthy
> This blessed house was founded, not for wealthy.
> He that endow'd for aye and this house builded
> By this good act hath to's sinne pardon yielded
> The honour of the country and this towne
> Alas now dead, his name was William Browne.
> Be it an house of prayer and to divine
> Duties devoted, else not called mine."

I was then privileged to be shown a most cherished possession—the original charter of the foundation, to which the seal of the Hospital is attached, and many other old charters, some of them dating from the reign of King John. In this connection I may add that Browne's Hospital is an " unreformed corporation," and only subject to its own government by the warden and pensioners, a distinction which it shares with St Cross, Winchester.

The cloisters are absolutely charming. They border a grass plot smooth as velvet, where croquet-hoops were set for the pleasure of the old folk. I saw two of the pensioners in their light gaiters, brown corduroy breeches, black coats and waistcoats with brass buttons, and tall silk hats. They reminded me for all the world of well-to-do country squires in past times—the type sometimes shown in musical comedy.

A raised terrace at the end of the garden that fronts their comfortable modernised quarters had a glowing border of roses and autumn flowers—golden-rod, asters, gladioli, Michaelmas daisies—a perfect blaze.

I left the peaceful retreat regretfully. I might have lingered there through the whole of that sunny afternoon had I not determined to visit All Saints' Church in the heart of the town. I wanted to see, before the light waned, the Browne family brasses, which I was told were most interesting.

I was well rewarded for my pains. Besides those in memory of his parents and other members of his family, I found two brasses in their original places over the graves where William Browne and Margaret, his wife, are buried. They are most delicately executed, and show him in a long gown standing upon two wool-packs. His wife wears flowing robes and has a dog at her feet. Elaborate canopies are engraven above their heads, as well as two labels—one inscribed " Me Spede " and the other " Dere Lady, help at nede."

The church abounds in old remains. On the wall there is a wrought-iron hour-glass stand, fixed near where the pulpit formerly was. Before the Restoration it was the practice to regulate the length of the sermon by means of an hour-glass.

A fine modern window, unusually pleasing in colour, was presented to the church by a Mr Browne of Boston, U.S.A., a descendant of William Browne, the founder of Browne's Hospital. Browne was a benefactor to this church as well as to his own Hospital.

Some other tiny houses of alms not far off are called the Callis House. They have recently been entirely rebuilt and now lack all architectural interest, but their name puzzled me until I learnt that it was probably derived from " Merchants of the Staple of Calais." These generous promoters of charitable foundations were wealthy wool merchants, who traded chiefly with the town of Calais. Amongst them we have already met with William Browne and his brother-in-law, Thomas Stokke. The whole town of Stamford, indeed, owes much of its well-being to this benevolent merchant, the continuance of whose good deeds gives the lie to Shakespeare's verdict that "The evil that men do lives after them ; the good is oft interred with their bones."

THE BEDEHOUSE, HIGHAM FERRERS

In the tiny village of Higham Ferrers exists a trilogy of ancient buildings, which I travelled from Stamford to see. They are the Bedehouse and school founded and endowed by Henry Chichele, Archbishop of Canterbury, and the church dedicated to the Virgin Mary. The memory of my visit is such a vivid pleasure that I must tell you of it, if only that you, too, may go and see likewise.

The village is unassuming as to its main feature—a compact little High Street, where old trees and old cottages rub shoulders with one another. But the colour of the place differs considerably from any of those I had at that time visited in Lincolnshire, or that I had passed through in Rutland and North-amptonshire itself.

The stone of which most of the dwellings are built is of a rich raw sienna in hue, varied now and then with stripes of creamy white. Creepers of all kinds seem to love it and cling to it affectionately, so that the patterned formality which might be displeasing is thus broken up, leaving only a cheerful impression of warmth.

When the blessed sun shines there, as it did on the

afternoon of my visit, a flame-coloured glow suffuses
the little place, putting the cool, tender tints of most
of our British hamlets to the blush, and calling to
mind the complexion of many a country homestead
in Italy or Southern France.

Passing through a gate, I came upon the old Bedehouse, the object of my pilgrimage.   It stood there
smiling in the sunshine, and next to it the charming
Vicarage.

Something about the homely, comfortable front of
the house inspired me with courage, so I rang the
bell, and was fortunate in gaining the favourable
ear of the Vicar.   He invited me into a dear little
old-world study, and I was soon confiding to him
my wish to make a more intimate acquaintance with
the Bedehouse and church.   The pleased alacrity
with which he rose to grant my favour was not only
proof of his kind hospitality, but showed clearly also
how dear to his heart were both church and almshouse.

First he took me into his garden, bordered on one
side by the south wall of the Bedehouse.   Here the
velvety turf was studded with fallen fruit—the too
luxuriant burden, golden and russet, of some ancient
apple trees.   The Vicar pointed out to me a beautiful
and very old ogee window at the far end of the wall—
a mellow wall with buttressed bays further enriched
by other and later Gothic windows protected by their
dripstones.

Then, through a glorious arched doorway we

entered the Bedehouse, and at once my eye was caught by the fine cedarwood six-bayed roof. The building no longer houses its colony of twelve pensioners, nor its bedeswoman who tended them. Their cubicles have been bricked up, though the traces are, of course, clearly to be seen. But the

The Bede House. Ogee Window. Higham Ferrers m.F.R.

men never fail to come and receive their weekly penny, and a bedeswoman now acts as caretaker. The Vicar fetched the dear old dame, who tripped along, wreathed in smiles, to see me. Formerly for many years, she told me, she had also had the care of the church, and it grieved her to the heart when ill-health compelled her to give up her charge. One could see that every stone of the ancient place was cherished by her. She spoke of it with as much pride

as many old ladies of their grandchildren. I asked
her if she would pose for me, and she kindly consented,
adding shyly :

" If you'd been a man, ma'am, I really couldn't
have ventured ! I'm so unused to visitors nowadays."

A fine stone hearth is on the right of the hall, and
some venerable oaken benches were placed along the
walls. When I was there, the rest of the furniture
consisted chiefly of easels holding school diagrams
and some framed drawings. The Vicar explained to
me that the hall is now used for meetings, readings,
and similar purposes. An old arch and screen
separate it from the small chapel, where services are
no longer held.

We next wandered out into the sunlit graveyard.
Beds of fragrant roses were set in the trimly cut
grass, and a tall memorial cross gleamed whitely. We
walked across to the church porch, splendidly preserved, and very interesting with its many arches and
carved stone-work.

The church itself is such a thing of beauty as to
rob one of words. Its spaciousness is what strikes
one first, for the aisles are almost as wide as the
nave, and the low, beautifully proportioned arches
increase the sense of width and space. There is
so much that is enthralling here that it is hard to
know of what to speak first. Primarily I ought to
mention the wonderful brasses. They are the finest
I have yet seen, and are reputed to be the memorials

of William Chichele and Beatrix his wife, the brother
and sister-in-law of Henry, Archbishop of Canterbury.

Bedeswoman.
Higham-
-Ferrers

The engraving is elaborate but very delicate, and the
design of the canopies above the heads of the graven
figures is marvellously graceful. I was told that

people come from all over the world to take the impress of these really delightful works of art. A very old brass of the first Vicar was also pointed out to me with pride. It dates from the eleventh century.

The church is further adorned by a fine Gothic screen, and a similar one in the north aisle, equally beautiful, is under process of repair. For its complete renovation, the Vicar told me, funds are urgently needed. The tracery of this decorated work is lovely beyond description. On the wall near the porch are placed two suits of armour, found, I heard, in the immediate neighbourhood. They are believed to have been worn by pikemen or guards of the late sixteenth century, and have been declared by experts to be most perfect specimens.

Standing apart, just outside the church on the right, is the schoolhouse, an exquisite little building. The varied but harmonious greys of its stone frontage, and its pierced parapet, through which the blue sky gleamed, remain in my mind—an unforgetable picture. Several of the fine Gothic windows were blocked up long ago, to protect the glass from the urchins' rough handling. But, nevertheless, when I entered it, the room was flooded with light from the large west window—its stone-work still quite intact.

Passing out again into the sunshine, I saw the old bedeswoman hurrying away, waving her hand to me, and the kind Vicar restraining his beautiful wolfhound, Peggy, near the Vicarage doorstep.

Meanwhile the shade deepened on the warm sienna and white of the Bedehouse and on the rich blue-greys of the school-building, and dusky indigo splashes of shadow picked out the carvings in the old arched porch of the church. The scene has left such a pleasant impression of bright and peaceful upliftedness, that I shall greatly look forward to paying Higham Ferrers another visit on some future day.

JESUS' HOSPITAL, ROTHWELL

AT Rothwell in Northamptonshire is a group of almshouses, known as Jesus' Hospital, of which the construction differs from that of any I have yet seen. It is divided into separate tenements. The oldest of these is dated 1591, and was founded by Owen Ragsdale, who came of a Nottinghamshire family.

Evidently he was born under a lucky star, for we glean from some old writings in the Hospital that he had the great fortune, when "but a youth and being of a good genius," to be chosen scholar of Magdalene College, Oxford, through the assistance of his uncle, Owen Ogglethorpe, at that time President of the College and later Bishop of Carlisle.

We are told that "for some time he plied his studies to very good purpose even till he went out Batchelour of Arts as soon as the University, for the sake of his ingenuity, had adorned him with that degree."

On the death of the bishop the people of Rothwell, or Rowel, as it was then called, begged Ragsdale to come to them. In the Grammar School there "he instructed the youth in learning and good manners," until he returned again to Oxford to study law. But soon after, inheriting property from an uncle in Yorkshire, he went back to Rothwell and married Mary Hamden, " a virtuous and frugal woman, and with a wife God gave him plenty of all things." Having no children, "he adopted poor persons and heirs." He had previously devoted some of his wealth to endowing the Grammar School and restoring the market to Rothwell, and had repaired the market-place at his own expense. He capped his good works by founding Jesus' Hospital, and Rothwell to this day holds him in the utmost veneration.

The Principal, who showed me over, drew my attention to a tablet let in above the door of the main entrance, on which is inscribed the following pious if rather original verse :

" God Bless our Governors prolong their days
   Who plac'd us here to render Heaven our prayers
     (? praise)
   To live contented, private and resigned
   Free from life's toils and humours of Mankind
   Pleased with wise Agurs (?) Mediocrity
   Too low for envy for Contempt too high
   What we now have we thankfully possess
   Till we exchange for greater happiness
        Henry Dormer Principal
           1721."

Passing upstairs, we entered, on the first floor, a common room shared by four men, which has a door in each corner leading to the cubicles. The Hospital was founded for thirty men, but only sixteen now inhabit it. I could not help feeling that the place lacked the womanly touch. The rooms seemed bare and rather comfortless, and I felt almost glad that there are no women-pensioners. The men are looked after by two attendants who, when necessary, combine the more prosaic calling of charwomen with that of nurses.

On this same floor there is a fine long room which originally served the purpose of a hall. Its old oak-barrelled roof and cornice, showing a delicate little beading right round the room, seem to constitute the building's chief claim to artistry.

I must confess to the weakness of an eerie qualm when the Principal beckoned me and whispered :

" Look here ! "

Bending down, he lifted an old iron ring in the floor, which raised a trap-door, cracked and worm-eaten with age. This revealed a rough, narrow, winding staircase leading down to a small chamber.

" Ugh ! " I said ; " that's quite gruesome."

" Yes, it does give you the creeps a bit, doesn't it ? " he answered ; " and so it ought ! It was used in former times as a prison or lock-up room when the pensioners were naughty boys. They were kept there on low rations till they had come to a right way of thinking ! "

He snapped the trap-door to and preceded me into a small room upstairs, formerly set apart, so he said, for the Principal's use. Here he pointed out to me the massive walls that were certainly over two feet thick.   Under the little window was a low seat, " for him to sit and read with the light behind his back—like this," explained my guide, suiting the action to the word.

Then we peeped into divers other rooms, some of them lined with cupboards.   One landing was graced with a good Jacobean balustrade, but its beauty had been hidden by a coating of whitewash.   On another landing the banisters had escaped this vandalism, and the surface of their original oak had been left undisturbed.

The Principal then led me to the back of the alms-houses, where the sight of the fine large gardens belonging to the pensioners quite cheered me.   Here they could, at least, enjoy nature and a wider outlook than is afforded to them within the four walls of their tenements.   Beyond the gardens is a goodly orchard where, this summer, the ripe fruit hung in rosy profusion.

" Do the old men reap the profits of the apple harvest ? " I asked my guide.

" Yes; they can sell the fruit if they like."

When, however, I contemplated the hundreds of apples and remembered that there are only sixteen decrepit and rather helpless old men to carry out the transaction, I am afraid I doubted whether they would make a good bargain.

On my way from the almshouses to the church I looked back at the imposing stone gateway with its name, 𝕵𝕰𝕾𝖀𝕾' 𝕳𝖔𝖘𝖕𝖎𝖙𝖆𝖑, engraved above it in Old-English letters. Under the arch stood one of the almsmen, an old bowed figure, in his top hat, dark blue coat and brass buttons.

Then, though it was growing late, I peeped into the church, and noticed three long pews set apart for the tenants of the almshouses. The first seat is allotted to the earliest inmate, the others following in due sequence, and a small pew adjoining is reserved for the Principal.

Ragsdale's stipulation in the Hospital code, that his "epitaph and superscription be kept whole, bright, and clean," drew me to seek out his tomb. Behind it, hanging on the wall, is a brass plate, framed in wood, showing his kneeling figure, hands clasped in prayer. On the left, going out of the church, I noticed a carved serpent, tail in mouth, supposed to be an emblem of eternity.

I must not forget to mention the Bone Crypt beneath the south aisle. Here, many years ago, were discovered the skulls and bones of innumerable corpses. The skeletons number from 30,000 to 40,000, and no one knows their history. One theory is that they are the remains of those who fell in the Battle of Naseby. If this be so, the dust of Round-heads and Cavaliers—erstwhile enemies—would seem at last to be indiscriminately mingled in peace.

Before leaving Rothwell I must tell you of one more outstanding feature which cannot be over-looked. Right in the heart of the town, in a large open square, stands the beautiful old Market House. It faces Market Hill, where the annual Charter Fair was held three hundred years ago, but, like other glories of the world, the fair has now vanished. The building, which was never finished, and part of which is now covered with lead to preserve it from the cruel onslaught of wind and weather, owes its inception to Sir Thomas Tresham in the fifteenth century. It is presumed that the architect may have been John Thorpe, to whom, in the reign of Elizabeth, many artistic and picturesque triumphs are ascribed, including Burleigh House, the noble home of the Marquess of Exeter. You will find I have alluded to this splendid achievement in writing about Stamford. A small round tower and staircase are seen at one side of the Rothwell Market House—a well-proportioned and symmetrical structure. A Latin inscription running round the building indicates the name of its author and the probable date of its erection —between 1575 and 1580. On high a succession of ninety shields decorates the parapet. One of these shields shows the pelican between three fleur-de-lys —the arms of Owen Ragsdale.

I was thus reminded that he had a hand in the construction of the three great architectural features of Rothwell, and it is little wonder that his name is venerated throughout the length and breadth of the town. He might, indeed, almost claim to be that rare exception, a prophet in his own country.

LORD BURGHLEY'S BEDEHOUSE, STAMFORD

In the heart of Stamford on the banks of the river
Welland—the picturesque stream that threads this
old town—stands a group of almshouses, of which
the present patron is the Marquess of Exeter.

The original founder, in the year 1170 or there-
abouts, was one Brand de Fossato. This noble man
deprived himself of all his possessions in order to
supply the means with which to establish the charity.
Of his foundation only two or three features remain.
They are, however, enough to impart a striking note
of age. They give value to the more modern edifice
that has been grafted on to them, and which we owe
to the benevolence of the great Lord Burghley. He
erected his Bedehouse in 1597 on the site of Fossato's
Hospital of St John and St Thomas.

An old water-arch and the pilastered buttress over
it are the only fragments left to us of the original
fabric, if we except a small Norman capital which
is built into the east wall in a queer inverted
position and adjoins the footpath winding along the
riverside. The remnants have, as we have already
seen, been embodied into Lord Burghley's later
structure.

From the other side of the water, the row of almshouses with their pointed gables and their diamond-
paned windows, fronted by a strip of green, add
much to the beauty of the river, which here flows
swiftly under the arches of old Stamford Bridge.

A small backwater runs under Fossato's Arch, but
then disappears utterly, and though I tried, I could
find no means of tracing its further current.   Perhaps
it rejoins the parent stream farther on.

A portly, pleasant dame in charge showed me one
of the little rooms.   Truth forces me to say that,
compared with many almshouses, the dwellings are
very meagre.   A tiny chapel has long since yielded
up all right to the name.

" I do my bit of ironing here and my washing-up,
for I look after the tenants, you know," said the
smiling matron.

One old fellow, peering round the door, added :

" And very kind she is to us too."

" Of course, ma'am," went on the matron confi-
dentially, " it couldn't have been treated this way
in past times.   Look at this old chest.   We pile the
dinner-plates on that !   And see this long table
here—a refectory table some of them call it.   I'm
told many set great store by a table like this.   Then
the old family escutcheons up there "—she pointed to
three mouldy coats-of-arms of the Cecil family,
spotted with damp and mildew.   " They ought to
look better than that, you know; but there," with
a shrug, " it's a mighty damp place, what with the

river running so near and all. You can tell that by the walls."

And indeed I could !

" My poor old folk, they mostly suffer from rheumatism ; but I think I make them happy in spite of it all."

" I'm sure you do," I said ; and then, by way of cheering her, I admired the long stretch of garden, full of brilliant autumn flowers, dividing the Bedehouse from the road.

" Oh, yes," she said, " the garden's fine and bright, isn't it ? And the men do take a pride in it. Did you happen to notice the ancient bell up there ? We don't often ring it now, but I reckon in the olden times it was used to call the bedesmen to prayers. Have you seen them on a Sunday, ma'am ? They're fine and smart then. They wear saxe-blue cloaks, very full, with flat capes, and the old badge in silver on them."

I promised to look out for them in their brave attire, and went my way reflecting that, after all, the present inmates have happier conditions than those of which we read in Miss Clay's *Mediæval Hospitals of England*. She tells us that one, Master Hugh, warden in 1299, defrauded the poor of their alms, locked up the rooms where strangers and sick should have been housed, and neglected the chapel.

The gay garden, the comely matron, and her contented old charges happily effaced this gloomy picture of the thirteenth century.

THE WATCH TOWER
JESUS HOSPITAL, LYDDINGTON

ABBEY FARM ALMSHOUSES
AUDLEY END

JESUS' HOSPITAL, LYDDINGTON

About twenty miles from Stamford, in the village of
Lyddington, is to be found another Bedehouse under
the patronage of the Marquess of Exeter. It has
fallen pitifully from its high estate, for it began life
in 1320 as a palace or country abode for the Bishops
of Lincoln. But in 1480 Bishop John Russell erected
the buildings which later, in the seventeenth century,
were turned into a Bedehouse by Thomas, second
Baron Burghley. At first the dwellings were organised to receive a warden, two poor women, and twelve
poor men. Now, however, only three old women are
tenants there.

From outside, the place is highly interesting with
its unusual facings of red brick and light stone-work.
A little octagonal watch-tower or gazebo, standing
at the end of the garden overlooking the highway,
first caught my attention. Five of its eight sides
project over the public footpath which runs beneath
its two arches. We are told that, in Bishop Russell's
time, it was probably embattled, and it once bore
his arms—a rose or, more significantly, a " roselle "
(Russell). But, alas, with the passing of time, unkind
wintry winds have done their worst, and scarcely a
trace of the emblem remains.

The Tudor windows of the Bedehouse, its groups of high chimneys, and, at the back, a cosy covered way with lean-to roof and sturdy oaken pillars, are most attractive. A mighty hornbeam, through whose thick foliage the sunlight filtered when I was there, dappling the grass below, added to the beauty.

I had written to the warden, who had made an appointment with me, but as there was no sign of him, one of the inmates kindly offered to fetch him from his work, and soon returned triumphantly in his company.

I was led up a narrow stone stairway to a landing where twin Gothic doors faced us. My guide opened the one on the right and ushered me into a most remarkable chamber. In olden times it was the bishops' dining-hall, and is very long, and lighted with several fine Gothic windows. Their stone-work is still intact, but the priceless old glass is, I grieve to say, in an advanced state of ruin. Here and there fragments, with admirably executed designs, still remain in their leaded frames, but for the most part cheap modern glazing has been substituted. I discovered a small, delicately traced head of Bishop Smith, one of the Bishops of Lincoln, but next to it, and in several other places, glass was missing altogether, and the gaps had been stuffed up with newspaper ! In winter, snow and rain must thus have free access, and the wind must howl and whistle through the crevices in a very creepy way.

The hall possesses a splendid flat oak ceiling

arranged in panels, and the beauty of its traceried
cornice, most delicately carved, filled   me with
admiration.   The sight of such exquisite and skilful
artistry conveyed the somewhat depressing truth
that we have progressed but little in all light
and graceful handiwork since the fifteenth century.
Probably in that very word, handiwork, lies the
reason of its excellence.   Nowadays we have only
time to turn out machine-made goods, and art such
as this dining-hall cornice at Lyddington is, alas,
too long for our short lives.   The greater the pity !

All the more reason why such precious relics should
be cared for and cherished, and it really seems
grievous to me that strips of this splendid frieze
are hanging, so to speak, by a thread, and are in
great peril of dropping to the floor.   *Verb. sat sap.*

I noticed in the hall an old trestle-table and forms,
and on the wall an illuminated panel giving a list
of the Bishops of Lincoln, and commencing with
Remicus (Remigius), 1072.

There is, too, a venerable oaken lectern, on which
rests the Lyddington Hospital Bible.   But what
interested me quite as much was the massive money-
box ; it is certainly two feet long, and so heavy that
I could not move it.   The warden told me that it
used to contain the fines of the bedesmen when they
failed to go to chapel.

As I left the hall, an old dame peeped out from
the twin door on the left and invited me into her
room.   She had contrived to make it look most

homely.   A piano stood against the wall, and a round table in the centre was loaded with the inevitable crowd of family photographs.   Tea was a-brewing. There was a nice fire on the ancient hearth, which,

Twin Doors. The Bede House Lyddington   m.F.R.

however, she said " smoked ter'ble," pointing to the blackened ceiling in proof of her words.

" Soon I expect a visit from my sister and brother-in-law from London," she confided to me, " so I've got these, for him to clean the cobwebs from the old beams here, and on the landing too."

She showed me two long canes something like fishing-rods.   The place certainly needed her rela-

tive's ministrations, for, like antique black lace, cobwebs, proofs of the spiders' unmolested industry,
hung in festoons from the rafters, grimy with soot.

The quiet churchyard, separating the Bedehouse
from the church of St Andrew, was robbed that day
of much of its mournfulness by a luxuriant weigelia
in full pink and white blossom.   I now crossed this
flowery ground to the church.

The tower and chancel would seem to be of the
fourteenth century, though the rest of the building
is Perpendicular.   Two old stone coffins with their
lids, which were found in the immediate neighbourhood and placed just inside the nave, are convincing
proofs of antiquity.

The chief characteristic of the structure which at
once attracted me is the position of the altar.   This
stands free, at a distance from the east wall, and is
surrounded by a complete square of old oak railings.
A pleasant impression is thus given of a furnished,
instead of a bare, space.   It is, I was told, a very
rare form of construction, and I have only come
across it once or twice before.

I had been particularly advised to take notice of
the acoustic jars.   These are placed high up in the
walls of the chancel, their open mouths level with
the surface—an ingenious plan adopted in olden
times to increase the auditory facilities of a place.

Two quaint old brasses lie near the altar.   On one
are to be seen the figures of Edward Watson and his
wife Emma.   She was the niece of the Bishop Smith

of whom I had discovered the little head in the Bede-house window.   Her husband was secretary to three of the bishops.   The Watsons must have been very proud of their progeny, for on either side of the memorial brasses, in the same metal, are diminutive groups of the couple's fifteen children—seven on one side and eight on the other.

Another brass shows the graceful figure of a woman, Helyn Hardy, who died in 1486.

The church had a fine carved-wood screen.   Of this the upper part is slightly restored, but below one can still discern traces of red and blue colouring. There is colour, too, far above, over the chancel arch, in some faint remains of frescoes.   It was impossible to make out the subjects they dealt with, and I was obliged to leave the church with my interest unsatisfied.   But so many features of the old place are engrossing, that I had plenty to ponder on my way home.

BUBWITH'S ALMSHOUSES, WELLS

LIKE many cathedral cities, Wells is endowed with several groups of almshouses. The most prominent of these is an interesting cluster of buildings founded by Bishop Nicholas Bubwith. He was, however, not destined to see the fulfilment of his good work, wherefore, in 1436, twelve years after his death, the erection of the almshouses was accomplished by his executors.

To Bishop Bubwith also, Wells Cathedral owes the creation of its north-west tower and the very beautiful chantry beneath which he is buried. He died on 27th October 1424, after having made his will on the 5th, and sealed and completed it on the 11th of that month. One cannot but envy the celerity of the proceeding. A striking contrast, indeed, to the more protracted methods of those who practise the law in our days !

His obsequies were attended by large numbers of the clergy and laity. A feast was prepared which must have been quite Lucullan in its appetising variety. In an old manuscript we may read minute particulars of the "funeral baked meats." There were three courses consisting in all of fifty-four dishes.

In the list we find, besides a wonderful variety of fish cooked in various ways, " Swan roste, Puddynge de Swan necke, Jollys (*i.e.* heads) of Salmon, Conning rostid (roast rabbit), Curlew, Yrchouns (some kind of preparation thickly studded with almonds, having something the appearance of a hedgehog), Crem of almaundys, Bakoun heryng, Blamangere."

Bubwith's Almshouses stand in Chamberlain Street near St Cuthbert's Church. It is a quiet and sequestered little street, quite different in character from the noisy High Street, which, when I was there, was literally infested with char-à-bancs. The almshouses seem to enjoy an almost monastic remoteness —the world forgetting, by the world forgot.

At once, the ancient porch attracted me. What a pity that the friable Bath stone shows unmistakable signs of having been too long exposed to many storms !

Passing down a small passage, I admired on my left a beautiful screen of old oak which shuts off the chapel.

I peered eagerly through its Gothic carving, which is charming and light in design, until the matron, seeing me, volunteered to unlock the door for me.

The ceiling of the chapel is quite unusual, and has ornamental circular beams combined with white plaster. The poppy-heads of the old pews are noteworthy, and, above all, I was fascinated by a queer

Bubwith's Almshouse
Wells

Almshouse
Moretonhampstead

little window in the east corner of the chapel, in
which have been assembled fragments of Bubwith's
coat-of-arms in rich old glass, with his name in
ancient lettering, as well as three other shields.
These shields, I was told, were removed from windows
in the common kitchen. On a corbel in the south
side of the chapel is a mitred head carved in stone,
with the initials N. B.; no doubt this represents
Bishop Bubwith.

We then went upstairs to the fine old hall in the
west end of the almshouses. Originally it was no
part of the establishment, but was used as a Guildhall
until 1779. A few years ago it underwent a further
change and was divided—one portion being set apart
for increasing the accommodation of the almshouses,
and the other part being devoted to the purposes of a
committee-room.

In the hall stands a very imposing piece—a unique
old deed chest in a quaint steel framework. The
coffer is gaily coloured, and the tints have remained
as fresh as if but recently painted. One of the
statutes for the government of Bishop Bubwith's
Almshouses requires "that there be a common
chest for safe keeping of the funds of the Hospital."
This ancient coffer is no doubt the original one used
for the purpose, though, from verses inscribed on
either end of it, the steel frame would seem to be of
a later date.

Leland says of the almshouse :

" Ther is an Hospitall of twenty-four poor menne

and wymen at the north side of St Cuthbert's Church. There is also a Cauntuary Priest.   The Hospitall and the Chapel is builded all in length under one roofe, from west to est.   Nicholas Bubwith, Bishop of Bath, was the founder of this, and brought it almost to perfection, and that that lakkid was completed by one John Storthwait, one of the executors of the Testament of Bubwith."

Old Deed Chest
Bishop Bubwith's Almshouses.   S! Saviour's Welk

Later the foundation was augmented by Bishop Still.   He must evidently have considered that the erection was not yet quite perfect, but " lakkid " something.   He therefore added a beautiful stone sedilia of the Cinquecento, which is now the most artistic portion remaining of the ancient building.

Above the chest in the hall, by the way, hangs a small engraving of this same Bishop Still with a round, kindly, placid face.   He was buried in the chancel of Hutton Church, where it is recorded that he

" dyed " in 1626. Over his tomb is the following epitaph :

> " Not that he needeth monuments of stone
> For his well gotten fame to rest uppon ;
> But this was reared to testifie that hee
> Lives in their loves that yet surviving bee
> For unto virtue who first raised his name
> He left the preservation of the same
> And to posterity remain it shall
> When brass and marble monumentes fall."

Another benefactor of the foundation was Bishop Williss. His additions, with those of Still, occupy adjacent buildings, and are tidily walled in together. They share a gay and pretty garden, where I saw tomatoes ripening and enjoyed the fragrance of a luxuriant myrtle bush, full of delicate little brush-like blossoms.

Here, too, resting on the sedilia aforementioned, I saw three old fellows, smoking and basking in the sunshine. A clothes-line had been slung from pillar to pillar of their fifteenth-century seat, and above it, on the line, were hung some practical if unpoetical nether garments of our prosaic twentieth century !

The snap-shotting of this characteristic group of inmates was irresistible. One of the trio stipulated that he should be presented with a print. They were all vastly elated at the notice taken of them, and they were graciously pleased to accept a small coin of the realm, in return for the favour they had granted of posing to me.

During the process the sun went in for a second, and by way of consoling me for this temporary check, one of the old men said :

" Don't you take on, ma'am ; he'll be back in a minute to see the fun."

The prophecy proved correct, and as I found my way home again to my inn, I had the pleasant recollection of those three smiling faces illumined by the friendly rays.

KING EDWARD VI'S ALMSHOUSES,
SAFFRON WALDEN

SAFFRON WALDEN is a delightful old town. With
its quaint timbered houses, many of them tastefully
colour-washed—I noticed one primrose, one pink,
one ochre, and others had trimmings of bright blue
and green—the place gives an impression of having
determined to strike an un-British note and adopt
the dress of some continental village. So deeply
did this fancy take hold of me that, throughout
my visit there, I had to remind myself I was on
English soil.

Truly I can imagine no pleasanter spot in which to
while away a week in the spring or summer. There
is a fine old parish church, parts of which remain from
the fourteenth century, and a stately mansion,
Audley End, the property of Lord Braybrooke.
This stands in charming grounds, and has a spacious
park through which there is a right-of-way, so that
all may enjoy its glorious trees.

The town can boast of historical remains dating
from Roman times, and it is adorned with several
picturesque old inns, one of which, the Sun, with
its quaintly plastered exterior, lingers particularly in
my memory.

213

Moreover, a beautiful picture gallery and a priceless little collection of old Italian and Dutch, as well as modern English, pictures is open to the public. It belongs to the Hon. Lewis Fry, and adjoins an idyllic seventeenth-century garden, deep-bosomed under shady trees. One could spend—how happily !—many hours musing amongst the graceful statuary and the queerly clipped shrubs of this old-fashioned pleasance.

Saffron Walden is indeed a fit spot for a poet or painter, and it was almost hard to tear myself away from all these attractions to visit the almshouses—the real object of my pilgrimage. But their history is also interesting, and well repaid me for what seemed at that time a sacrifice.

They were founded by Roger Waldine, Archbishop of Canterbury in 1400, and were re-established by Edward VI in 1550 after the Dissolution.

The Dame, as the matron is called, took me over the building. She is a delightful cheery woman, who made the welkin ring with her good-humoured laughter. She declared she was proud to show me " the glories," or so she named them, of " her place."

The comfortable modern cottages house thirty-eight aged couples of good character, the only stipulation being that would-be tenants must have resided for at least ten years in Saffron Walden.

An authentic and well-painted portrait of Edward VI hangs over the chimney in the hall to which she led me. Here I also saw a fine refectory table and a couple of old benches, and on the walls two massively carved brackets, which were brought indoors from the open air for their safer keeping. The inventory of the almshouses is to be seen there as well, and some of the entries are very quaint. I jotted down the following :

" vii Spittes and a greate braze Pott.   iii drippinge panes, ii great cobbernes.   In the hall iij Tabeles, a lictorne to laye on bookes, a payer of Schales and a pound of brazen waiytz, item a great troff to knede in."

In an old book lent to me, I found besides that—

" The executors also left in hall a bacyn and a lavour, a banker (a bench), and a doser (probably dossier, the back of a chair), iiij trestlys and ij mete tablys ; and in the buttery two barrelys for ale, two bord clothys, iiij lave napys and a towayle, vi sponys of the weight of x shillings and a maser price xls, the which maser Margaret Breychman gaf to serve in the forseyd house perpetual for the souls of her and Stephen Breychman and all her frendys."

The Dame told me that in former times Saffron Walden was noted for the brewing industry, and the inmates used to brew their own beer.   She showed me the brewhouse, with its stove that runs the whole length of one wall.   At Christmas the old people used to be given a pailful of beer and four faggots.

The Dame was justly proud of the extensive

gardens and orchard of the almshouses, and drew my attention to an ancient barn that had been roofed over for drying purposes.

The most valued possession of the institution is its mazer bowl, mentioned above, and dated about 1400. It is now kept in the bank for safer custody. This precious treasure I was privileged to see. Pepys, in his *Diary* under date 1659, when visiting Walden, says :

" In our going my Landlord carried us through a very old hospital or almshouse, where forty poor people were maintained ; a very old foundation ; and over the chimney-piece was an inscription in brass : ' Orate pro anima Thomae Bird ' etc. (the Vicar of Much Munden in 1490). They brought me a draft of their drink in a brown bowl, tipt with silver, which I drank off, and at the bottom was a picture of the Virgin with the Child in her arms done in silver."

The foundation of King Edward VI's Almshouses has been considerably augmented by the generosity of the Gibson family, and one of its members now presents ten shillings every Christmas to each old person. For this ceremony the celebrated mazer bowl is fetched from the bank to hold the doles, and the lady distributes them, no one else being allowed to touch the valuable object.

By the bye, it is interesting to know that the bowl is insured for the sum of £2000. A year or so ago, when lent to an exhibition, it was even insured for

£3000, and one of those responsible for it told me that he only breathed again when it was safely returned !

Besides the almshouses of Edward VI at Saffron Walden, in the hamlet of Audley End, close by, are some very picturesque and curious tenements of brick. They probably date from the fifteenth century, and are called the Abbey Farm, or Lord Braybrooke's Almshouses. They are the remains of the infirmary or hospital of a vanished monastery, established in 1136 by Geoffrey de Mandeville, and no doubt the original foundations lie beneath the lawns of Audley End. At a later period, Thomas, first Earl of Suffolk, made some allowance to the inmates, and the building is described in the parish register as " My Lord's Almshouse." But it appears that his widow discontinued the payments when she got into financial difficulties, for Mr Garrard, writing in 1663 to the Lord Deputy of Ireland, says :

" The Countess of Suffolk is run away, or hid herself so that she cannot be found, because she refuses to pay £1400 arrear. . . . She pretends poverty and I believe is so, for she has dissolved her husband's Hospital at Audley End, not being able to maintain it any longer. Serjeants-at-arms seek her daily, but she cannot be found."

The place was originally built for ten old women, but now only three are housed there. It still possesses a fine carved oak fireplace, and in some of the windows can be seen portions of old glass.

With its cobble-stoned courtyards in which the
grass grows unheeded, and its old quadrangle where
ivy has thrown an eclipsing veil, the Abbey Farm
is to-day, alas, nothing but a picturesque relic of
old-world beneficence.

ST BARTHOLOMEW'S HOSPITAL, NEWBURY

In the old town of Newbury I happened, quite by chance, on a very ancient block of almshouses, humble yet very snug, lying back behind their gay little flower-gardens. I ascended stone steps and, greatly venturing, opened a gate flanked by pilasters.

One of the old dames came out to me, anxious to do the honours. With her I passed through an archway forming the centre of the dwellings. It is surmounted by an ancient clock-tower, and she proudly pointed out to me an inscription at the rear stating that the foundation was created by King John in 1215.

Under the archway stands an aged and worm-eaten bench, on which no doubt many generations of tired tenants must have rested.

Across the road is an old house, most attractively set amidst gnarled and venerable trees. It goes by the name of St Bartholomew's Manor House, and bears a thirteenth-century date.

Later I came upon further evidence of the early foundation of the Hospital, to which are affiliated those of Upper and Lower Raymond.

I found, in fact, that the historian, Gervase of Canterbury, in his *Mappa Mundi*, which he must

have compiled soon after 1200, includes St Bartholomew's in his list of well-known Berkshire hospitals.

The original charter is wanting, but in the Close
Rolls mention is made of the grant of a fair, showing
that the institution received the King's favour as
early as 1215 :

> "The King to the Sheriff of Berkshire—
> Greeting. Know that We have granted to the
> Hospital of St Bartholomew at Newbury and
> to the brethren serving God there, that they
> may have each year a fair at Newbury lasting
> two days—that is to say, on the day and on
> the morrow of St Bartholomew's Day. Pro-
> vided however, that such fair shall not be to
> the injury of neighbouring fairs.
>
> "And therefore We order you that you allow
> the said Hospital and the aforesaid brothers to
> have the aforesaid fair for two days, together
> with all its appurtenances and liberties and free
> customs belonging to fairs of this kind as afore-
> said.
>
> "Witness myself at Ciren(cester) the 7th day
> of July (1215)."

It is a far cry from 1215 to 1926. The brotherhood
and their fair are no more, but the Hospital of St
Bartholomew still stands stolidly on its ancient site.

THE ALMSHOUSES OF SHAFTESBURY

CROWNING the ridge of a chalky range of Dorset downland—a ridge that in another county expands into the Chiltern Hills—is the little town of Shaftesbury, set like the central jewel of a queen's diadem. From afar as one threads Dorset's leafy valleys, one spies the ancient place dominating miles of surrounding country. The road winds up and up, past half-timbered cottages and stone barns, and at last develops into the quaint high street of the old town.

A venerable church, which was fortunate in having escaped from Cromwell's depredations, stands at the summit. It is still beautiful in its sturdy strength, though the carving of its stones is sadly worn here and there by the inroads of wind and weather that must assail it often at that exposed height.

Shaftesbury owns two sets of almshouses. One— Chubb's Almshouses, in Salisbury Street, built to house sixteen women—was disappointing. I was on the look-out for the brass plate, spoken of by Hutchins. It is, he writes, over the door, and bears the inscription :

" Anno Dom. 1611 Matthew Chubb, of Dorchester, gent. was the founder of this house and Margaret his widow gave some maintenance unto it."

Old Shaftesbury. M.F.R.

But nothing remains now of this old plate. Instead, a panel outside the house gives the rather bald intimation: " Chubb's Almshouse 1811, rebuilt by the Corporation 1834."

Across the road a little farther on is a much more satisfactory building—at least from the antiquarian's point of view—Spiller's Almshouse. Its picturesque front pleased me greatly. This, too, used to bear a coat-of-arms and a plate on which was graven :

DONUM DEI ET DEO. ANNO DOMINI 1660.

A stone below shows the further inscription :

" SPILLER'S SPITTLE. 1656.

" Sir Henry Spiller, of Laleham, Co. Middlesex, Knt."—evidently a kindly and generous person— " in his lifetime being desirous to leave a perpetual testimony of his affection to the borough of Shaston " (the local name for Shaftesbury), "the place of his birth, and to manifest some act of charity for the relief of ten poor men . . . the most aged and impotent of the said borough" . . . left certain lands . . . " for the building of an almshouse, or Maison de Dieu, in or near the street called Salesbury Street."

A common room erected by a former Marquess of Westminster adjoins the rooms of these ten needy men. Wandering a little way beyond the old church, I came upon a fine plateau or terrace called Park Walk. Here I sat and enjoyed a timely cigarette under one of the row of glorious ancient beech trees. Below me spread fold upon fold of swelling hills and pastured dales, through which here and there I caught gleams of the silver Stour.

At the foot of the plateau, clustering together in

time-honoured intimacy, are the russet, moss-grown roofs and spires of the tiny parish of St James. Here was once to be found the now vanished "Dolhouse," or Magdalen's (Maudlin's) Almshouse. I spent amongst these old houses some time in the futile endeavour to trace this building, but met everywhere with the disheartening assurance that it had been "done away with years ago." Probably the inhabitants of the townlet of Shaftesbury, perched serenely on its hill-crest, decided that two sets of almshouses amply filled its needs. Be that as it may, the town has not replaced the third and missing group. The two remaining abide there, peacefully conscious of the beauty of their surroundings and of the fair view at their feet.

Lyford Almshouses

THE ALMSHOUSES, LYFORD

A LOVELY June afternoon tempted me from Abingdon, where I was staying, to investigate the little village of Lyford, some six or seven miles away. I had heard that it possessed attractive almshouses of the Jacobean period, and any excuse for a quest would have been plausible on such a delightful day, when everything was singing a joyous pæan of early summer.

By contrast with the splendid dwellings of a similar kind I have met with, the Lyford Almshouses seemed to be but homely country cousins. Those two pleasing rows of little cottages, gay with flowers and with recently renewed green-painted doors, smiled at one another with cheerful rusticity across a broad cobble-stoned pathway.

At the entrance, next to a couple of brick pilasters, high bushy yews stood steadfastly sentinel. Their blue duskiness struck a dense cool note in the midst of all the brightness. A few hundred yards along the road I noticed the Vicarage gates, and in front of these streamed festoons of brilliant flags. It was easy to see that some sort of local fête was in progress.

Along that sunny bit of road the village community, festively arrayed, wended its way. Indeed, at that very moment the big drum, its owner obviously late and warm, hurried past me on a motor-bike.

Several of the almshouse dames were foregathered in front of their cottages, evidently adorned for the fray. Though I was very curious to know the reason for all this gaiety, my mind misgave me that I had happened on the scene at an inopportune moment.

One of the buxom old souls came excitedly towards me.

" We've a fête in the Vicarage grounds," she explained. " I declare I thought you were Lady ——. She'll be along in her car at any moment."

At which, of course, I offered to make myself scarce, but I was told—

" Oh, no, you can look around, mum, if you will excuse me, as I must go along."

Another old party and her husband, however, came forward and offered to take me over the gardens —prolific plots of vegetables and flowers of which the tenants seemed justly proud.

The foundation of the almshouses, I had read, was of the year 1611, though I am bound to say I could detect nothing to date the epoch, unless it were the small chapel at the far end—now temporarily out of use. These ancient foundations generally had chaplains of their own, but the present occupants of the almshouse attend the local church.

The couple told me that the houses harbour sixteen souls, and are nice and cosy.

Fearing to be a nuisance at this eventful moment,

I now bid them a tactful farewell. I was soon skimming along the lanes on my homeward journey through gentle pastureland, golden with buttercups and ethereal with the dreamy whiteness of wild hemlock. Above me, adding fragrance, the May trees still spread their snowy blossom. The air was vocal with the song of birds, and only a rare waggon or car disturbed for a moment the prevailing peace. I must confess to a feeling of smug content when I thought of that poor, overheated performer on the big drum.

ST MARGARET'S HOSPITAL, WIMBORNE

In the neighbourhood of Wimborne are two alms-houses. The first, St Margaret's Hospital, has the paramount claim to attention by reason of its age, although the Hospital of Wimborne St Giles is, to my mind, the more picturesquely attractive.

Studying the histories of our old houses of alms, one learns that as the fell disease of leprosy died out, the leper-houses were converted into almshouses, or, as they were also called, hospitals.

One of the first of these was St Margaret's, a benevolent survival, seven hundred years old. For some time John of Gaunt was supposed to have been its founder, but afterwards we read that the foundation was due to a Duke of Acquitaine and Lancaster in the early thirteenth century.

Hutchins, in his *History of Dorset*, tells us that "About a quarter of a mile to the north-west of the town of Wimborne stands an hospital or almshouse with a small chapel belonging to it, dedicated to God, St Margaret, and St Anthony. The time of the foundation is entirely unknown, but by many curious ancient deeds, donations, and evidences . . . one of which . . . appears to have been written as far back as the reign of King John and is still fair and legible, it is evident that this hospital was then in being."

After a drive, I found all too short, through the pleasant vales and lanes of Dorset, I reached Wimborne, and lost no time in going to St Margaret's.

The little chapel there drew me at once. In a brief account, framed and hung within its walls, I read that the original endowment had "neither lands nor goods to maintain it, but only the charitable alms of the people." "One William Crofte," it adds, "was elected and chosen to be proctor of the said hospital and to show the people the great indulgents and pardon that is granted to all benefactors of the said hospital and to receive and gather such alms as they may be disposed to give."

One hopes, by the way, that William Crofte was of the genial type of agent, so that the benefits he dispensed were sweetened to the recipients' palates, for we know that the flavour of charity is sometimes bitter.

Hutchins also quotes from an old deed that "Pope Innocent IV in the year 1245, by an indulgence or bulle did assoyl them of all signs forgotten, and offences done against fader and moder, and all swerynges neglygently made. This indulgans, granted of Petyr and Powle, and of the said Pope, was to hold good for fifty-one years and two hundred and sixty days, provided they repeated a certain number of Paternosters and Ave Marias daily."

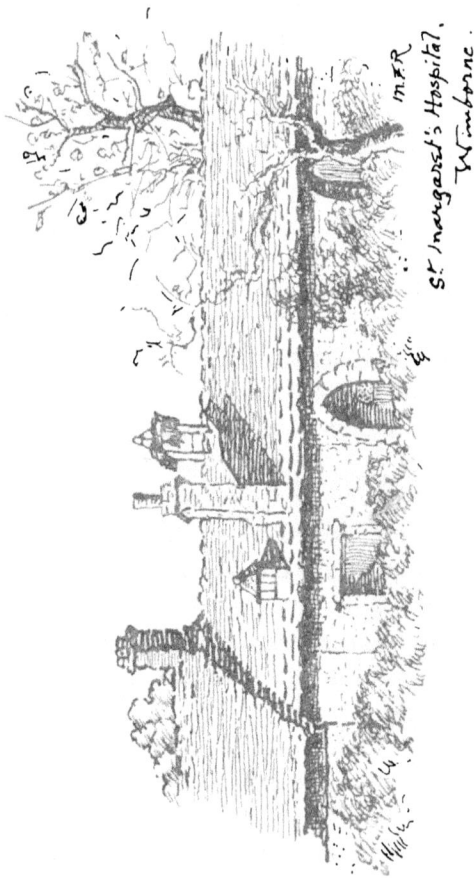

St. Margaret's Hospital.
Wimborne.

The dwellings, of which eleven are now occupied, are clustered about an open garden in groups of two and three.   Each has a little plot of its own, and at the time of my visit the pink buds of flowering currant were already visible, and the young green spears of the daffodils' leaves had pierced the dark mould.

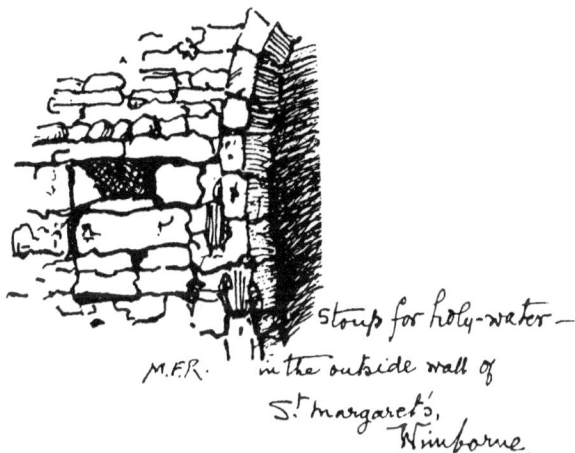

Stoup for holy-water —
in the outside wall of
St. Margaret's,
M.F.R.   Wimborne.

It was evident that the patient care of the owners would soon be repaid by a wealth of flowers.

To the left is the chapel, and here the sick and infirm of the neighbourhood come to worship on Thursday afternoons, when service is held by one of the clergy of Wimborne Minster.

The interior of the chapel looks very fresh and clean, for it has been lately renovated, but the furbishing has been done with great tact, so that the architectural beauties have been piously preserved.

The roof is an open one, showing the ancient beams, and to the walls still cling remnants of bygone frescoes. Three of the doors seen on the north side are pointed, and on the left of the one leading into the porch is an old stoup for holy water, which I have sketched. It is an unusual feature, for it is not often that these stoups are found on the outside of the building.

In the south wall of the chapel is a little lancet window, and in the roof above it are three courses of large stones. At one time the entire roof was covered with them. I yearned for a nearer view of the south side. So I knocked at one of the cottage doors and asked permission of an old almsman, whom I surprised at his toilet, to pass through his cottage to the garden beyond. His deshabille was certainly obvious, but nothing daunted, towel in hand, he showed me into his room—a very cosy one, where family photographs graced the walls and brass utensils shone bravely.

St Margaret's Hospital has an air of orderly comfort. It is quite clear that, however impoverished its early days may have been, it now enjoys a modest affluence, and its inmates are fortunate to be so snugly housed for the remainder of their earthly span.

ALMSHOUSES
WIMBORNE ST. GILES

HALL'S ALMSHOUSES
BRADFORD-ON-AVON

THE HOSPITAL OF WIMBORNE ST GILES

FROM St Margaret's Hospital it is easy to pass on to the cheerful little almshouses of Wimborne St Giles, about eight miles to the north.

Even the road leading to them is full of the rural felicities in which Dorset abounds. The small river Allen threads its happy way through undulating meadows. Here and there—the month being fill-dyke February when I was there—it had broken bounds like a refractory school-urchin, and had spread itself into tributary streams where the blue of the sky was brightly mirrored. Bordering the road, thick yew hedges tell a tale of age. That morning the sun was kind, and the lattice windows of venerable thatched cottages twinkled in its light. Birds were busying themselves in the leafless branches, and some precocious lambs browsed peacefully in the fields by their mothers' sides.

The hamlet of Wimborne was first called Upwinborne, but later took to itself the name of St Giles, from the dedication of its church.

At first I was quite puzzled to find the almshouses. They lie back from the winding road and look out upon a spacious green. A little to their right the

village school stands sentinel, while the old church of
St Giles protects them on their left. Beyond the
green, and sloping down to it, is a copse, just then
still dusky in its winter austerity. The whole forms,
so to speak, a little dale encircled by gentle uplands.

The almshouses consist of ten dwellings, five on
each side of a recessed porch, but the tenth now serves

An Avenue. Near Wimborne

as the church vestry, having been chosen for this
purpose when the interior of the church was destroyed
by fire in 1908. The other nine houses are still in
the gift of the Shaftesbury family, and are occupied
by widows and widowers. The porch has a fine old
carved door of the Tudor period that leads into a
chapel no longer used. Above, cut in stone, stand
the words :

LIBERASTI ME DOMINE
IN MAXIMA TRIBVLATIONE.

Higher still, also in stone, though somewhat defaced by time and rough weather, are the Shaftesbury arms.

Along the whole length of the dwellings runs a delightful paved walk of old red bricks, enclosed by a low moss-grown wall. It protects a wide flower-border from the cutting winds. When I saw the place, primroses, snowdrops, and wall-flowers were beginning to bloom, and a vigorous bush of japonica was already rosy with blossom. A gnarled and mighty wistaria had festooned itself across the old porch, and climbing rose-bushes clung to the walls.

At one end of the terrace is the pump—an indispensable commodity—and at the other is the church. It holds the monument of Sir Anthony Ashley, the founder of the almshouses, who died in 1627.

The present church dates from 1732, and stands on the site of two earlier ones, of which but a few remnants are left to tell the tale. John de Fissa is recorded in 1207 as the first rector. In 1291 the church became known as the Chapel of St Giles.

Some of the inmates were sunning themselves on the terrace, and one old dame bade me "kindly enter," and displayed a charming living-room. The ubiquitous portrait of Queen Victoria hung there, dominating the room, and an ancient warming-pan and a pink lustre teapot rubbed shoulders with a gramophone of the horn variety.

"Ah, ma'am," said the old lady, patting it thoughtfully, " 'tis dumb now. I haven't had the heart to set it going since my husband died."

I was able to snap a group of the inmates. One of the old dames happened to have a purse in her hand.

" Lor ! " she said, popping it in her pocket, " it won't do for that to be seen in the picture, or they'll say I'm rich and hadn't no right to be here ! "

Old Stocks -
Wimborne
St. Giles

A little farther along the road, as one leaves St Giles, stand the ancient and decrepit stocks, now protected by a small penthouse and railing. Considering the advanced state of dilapidation to which these restraining tools of law and order are reduced, it is lucky that, like Othello, their occupation is gone. In their present condition they would be but frail

implements indeed on which to count for the castiga-
tion of wrong-doers !

Near by is the village signboard, showing St Giles
and his doe. The saint is removing from the beloved
beast the arrow that had been sped by Royal command. I had become acquainted with his history
in the old French town of St Gilles in Provence, and
I remembered that he was the patron saint of all
rustic life.

Perhaps that was why the nests of two robins had
been built in the chancel of the little Wimborne
church, where they were afterwards discovered.
No doubt the robins knew they would be safe in a
spot dedicated to him !

NAPPER'S MITE, DORCHESTER

HAVING read that Napper's Mite, Dorchester, was a charming little building of the early seventeenth century, my anticipations ran high when I started out to visit it. The town, too, I knew must have an interesting history, for is it not the capital of Dorset, and has not Thomas Hardy's pen immortalised it as Casterbridge? Even the weather, a factor to be reckoned with on such excursions, seemed to be favouring the jaunt, and the sweeping Dorset uplands and inviting lanes, where birds sang among the branches just breaking into leaf, all welcomed me that sunny spring morning.

But I must frankly own that I was destined to be disillusioned. I made my way to South Street, where I had learnt that I should see Napper's Mite, which was founded in 1615 by Sir Robert Napier of Middlemarsh Hall.

And true enough, there in Dorchester's chief thoroughfare it stands, as the inscription over the door testifies. But it is wedged in between high warehouses and modern shops, and a careless throng of busy folk, intent on their own affairs, hurry past it unconcernedly. Familiarity with its quaint little exterior has possibly bred contempt in the eyes of

238

its daily beholders, so that it shares the fate of the prophet who is without honour in his own country.

At any rate, the building seems to strike a derelict note, in spite of its attractive and well-preserved old arcade and its little stone arches on either side of the doorway. With Wimborne St Giles and other cosy houses of alms fresh in my mind, the whole place to me had a forsaken look, and, after knocking twice in vain, I was just turning away, when the door was opened and an apologetic dame of meagre aspect appeared who asked my business.

She ushered me through a dark passage into a small dismal courtyard. Its depressing aspect was intensified by a few grimy bushes, bravely struggling to live between cracked and broken paving-stones.

Standing in this make-shift for a garden, the old woman informed me that she and seven men, of whom the youngest was seventy-nine, inhabited Napper's Mite, and that they received six shillings a week. She also pointed out the disused chapel where hung Sir Robert Napier's coat-of-arms in stone, with the inscription:

LA MITE NAPPIER

BUILT TO THE HONOUR OF GOD

BIE SIR ROBERT NAPPER, KNIGHT,

ANN

XENODOCHIUM.

This last word, Mr Sidney Heath tells us, signifies in Greek " a hospital for strangers," and also defines the date of the foundation MDCXV. Formerly this slab had its place on the outer wall of the almshouse.

Ascending a crazy staircase, I was surprised by an upper apartment of roomy and spacious dimensions.

" This," said my guide, " used to be the guest-room." She sniffed apologetically at its unwelcoming aspect.

" Well, it must have been a beautiful room once," I replied, " but I must confess that in its present state I'd rather be excused its hospitality. What a pity the powers that be should have allowed it to fall into such disuse ! "

The old woman opened a cupboard and drew my attention to the works of the large round clock, which I had already noticed in the street, on an ornamental bracket over the entrance door of the almshouse. On a shelf outside the guest-room I caught sight of an ancient prayer-book, across which spiders, undisturbed, had woven their webs—a silent proof of dusty abandonment !

As I was leaving, one of the occupants appeared in the doorway of his room. His smiling, rosy face was the most cheering sight I met inside Napper's Mite. He begged me to peep into his domain, and was loud in praise of its comfort. I quitted the almshouses directly afterwards, hurrying away so that his contentment should be my last memory in connection with Sir Robert Napier's gift to Dorchester.

CHARTERHOUSE (OR SUTTON'S HOSPITAL), LONDON

BURIED in the busy heart of London, in a little quiet corner near a main artery of the city, lives, secluded within ancient flint-stone walls, one of the most interesting relics of early English times, the Charterhouse, or Sutton's Hospital. I say designedly lives, for, despite the passage of six centuries, the building abides, sturdy and virile, apparently defying the ruinous hand of time.

Beneath the old place rumbles at all hours of the day, and half the night, the Underground Railway, conveying the seething population to and fro from every quarter of the London world. Hard by thunder huge motor-lorries, drays, and vans, pursuing their steady business. The coming and going of hundreds of schoolboys from the adjacent Merchant Taylors' School, the shrieking of hooters, and even yet, the clatter of horses' hoofs along those streets where cobble-stones have still survived the ubiquitous asphalt—all this clamour and much more leaves the repose of the Charterhouse undisturbed.

The quiet of its present existence offers a strange contrast to the stress of its birth and early days.

Let me tell you how it came into being.

In the middle of the fourteenth century the plague —a terrible scourge from remote Asia—swept across Europe, reaching England at the end of 1348. The churchyards of London were soon overfilled, and things were in a ghastly plight till Ralph Stratford, Bishop of London, took the matter in hand and bought three acres of ground, then known as No-Man's-Land, but later called Wilderness Row. In this spot he installed and consecrated a new burial-place.

His grand example was soon followed by Sir Walter de Manny, a noble gentleman of France, of whom we must talk later. He added to the bishop's another gift of a much larger plot, and here 50,000 victims of the pestilence were buried.

De Manny's piece of ground belonged to the brothers of Bartholomew's Spittle, and measured thirteen acres and a rod. Sir Walter must indeed have been an adept in the practices of charity, for he had intended to enlarge the scope of his benefits by further gifts, but instead he was called away to the war to defend his own country. He therefore sold his London property to Michael de Northburgh, who had meanwhile succeeded Stratford as Bishop of London. In 1361, however, the project suffered a serious hindrance—*festina lente*—Northburgh died.

True, he left nearly all his wealth to found a monastery for twenty-four Carthusian Friars, and the good deed was at length accomplished ten years afterwards, when Sir Walter de Manny undertook to erect and endow the monastery. And now I will give you a few hasty details of Sir Walter's life, for he was a notable figure among the many that crowded the gallant times in which he lived. Besides, was it not of him that the great chronicler, Froissart, wrote : "He did so many prowess in divers places, that it were hard to make mention of them all " ?

He hailed from the province of Hainault, and was born in the town of Manny, of which he was lord. He has left a glowing memory there, his bravery and high bearing, while fighting for his own land, having brought him great renown.

Later, his countrywoman, Philippa of Hainault, came to England to marry King Edward III. De Manny formed one of her train, and Edward, quick to recognise the nobleman's worth, honoured him with a knighthood.

Sir Walter was present at the famous siege of Calais and, with Queen Philippa, interceded for and saved the lives of the French hostages.

When he was an old man he returned to England and, as we have seen, began to carry out de Northburgh's project. But in 1372 death—the supreme arbiter—again cut short man's noble efforts. We read that de Manny " was buried with great pomp in the monastery, his funeral being attended by the King, his children, and the barons and prelates of England."

A portion of Sir Walter's tomb, carefully cherished

in a glass case, was shown to me. The tomb had been discovered by a workman when engaged on repairs, and one can well picture his excitement at the " find," for the fragment is gay with bright colours, undimmed by age. No doubt the rest of the monument might have been disclosed—and, like Oliver Twist, one craves for more—but, as my guide, the head porter, sagely remarked, it would not do to pull down the whole Charterhouse on the chance! De Manny, by the bye, was, I was told, the original of Conan Doyle's Sir Nigel Loring in *The White Company*.

The monastery prospered until the Dissolution, then it became the property of Lord North, and later, as we shall learn, of the fourth Duke of Norfolk. To each of these it owes some features of beauty that still survive and help to recall its history.

One of its owners was created Earl of Suffolk by James I, and from the earl it was bought in 1611 by good old Sir Thomas Sutton, a wealthy merchant, who endowed it as a hospital for forty poor boys and eighty poor men. But fate is often a grim satirist, and death overtook the kindly founder before the work was finished. On its completion, however, in 1614, a picturesque tribute was paid to him, for in the flickering light of many torches that emphasised the rich gloom of the chapel, his body was solemnly carried to its last resting-place by the poor brothers he had so generously benefited.

The endowment still exists, though the brothers

are now reduced to fifty-nine, because, as my guide said, " times are bad."

As to Charterhouse School, its growth should relieve the minds of pessimistic educational reformers. Not many years ago it was moved to Godalming.

Doorway. Charterhouse.
M. FR.

The number of its scholars, as years went by, had quite outgrown the capacity of the London building. This was then pulled down and the Merchant Taylors' School erected on its site.

Near the Gatehouse—now the porter's lodge—is a glorious old gate. One enters at once into the Master's Court, where, on the right, is the house now inhabited by the Master of Charterhouse, Dr Gerald

Davies, to whom we owe much valuable information about it. Quite lately, too, its full history by the late Sir William St John Hope has been published.

The main building owes the addition of this wing to Thomas Howard, fourth Duke of Norfolk. He installed himself at Charterhouse in the sixteenth century, and made it his chief home. It must, indeed, have been a very beautiful one, for he enlarged as well as greatly improved it. Possibly he meant to convert it into a Royal abode, for we are told that while living there he aspired to the hope of marriage with Mary, Queen of Scots. After all, one asks oneself, why not ? Mary Stewart—the alluring, the irresistible—had many admirers. If Norfolk were one of them, surely it was, so to speak, only the desire of the moth for the star !

In more halcyon days who knows whether he might not have lived, an Emperor or some such brilliant butterfly-consort, rather than, moth-like, have folded fluttering wings in death ? But destiny decided otherwise and favoured a rival star, who outshone his constellation. And thus his plan, if plan it were, went agley, like many another best laid one. Queen Elizabeth got wind of it, and promptly clapped him into the Tower for twelve months. Freed again, he is said to have renewed his wooing. We must guess, however, that our English Queen's basilisk eye was upon the lovers, for their secret correspondence was traced, and in 1571 Norfolk was again imprisoned. Then, no doubt, at Charterhouse an exhaustive search for further damning proofs was made. And indeed, hidden away there, beneath the tiles on the roof, what should be found but the key to some letters written in cypher! On their evidence and that of other correspondence Norfolk was tried, convicted of treason, and executed in 1572. His aspiring wings would never soar again.

Leaving the Master's Court, I passed into a cloister leading to the chapel. There is a tablet inscribed with the names of the priors and masters of the monastery. The first is that of John Luscott, who held the post of prior in 1371. But there are, besides, other tablets here, doing honour to great men connected with Charterhouse. These memorials commemorate Thackeray, Leech, Sir Henry Havelock, Wesley, Roger Williams, the founder of Rhode Island, U.S.A., and other eminent Carthusians. But I must own that to me the name whose lustre dims all the others is that of Thackeray.

Thackeray! He came to school here! And that fact alone glorifies for me the soil on which Charterhouse stands. The following passage describing the ancient place will be familiar to all his readers :

" . . . There is an old Hall, a beautiful specimen of the architecture of James' time ; an old hall ? many old halls ; old staircases, old passages, old chambers decorated with old portraits, walking in the midst of which, we walk as it were in the early seventeenth century."

Yes, indeed ! In *The Newcomes*, Charterhouse as

Grey Friars has been immortalised by Thackeray. I cannot resist quoting for you the delightful passage treating of Founder's Day :

" The boys are already in their seats, with smug fresh faces, and shining white collars ; the old black-gowned pensioners are on their benches ; the chapel is lighted, and Founder's Tomb, with its grotesque carvings, monsters, heraldries, darkles and shines with the most wonderful shadows and lights. There he lies, Fundator Noster, in his ruff and gown, awaiting the great Examination Day."

As I followed my guide through the wonderful place, the beloved figure of the Colonel, so familiar from endless readings of Thackeray's incomparable book, seemed to accompany me. I could almost see the spare form in its long black brother's gown, the noble old head with its twinkling deep-set eyes, the fine aquiline nose, the bushy side-whiskers, the gaunt, soldierly figure wearing with martial dignity, and thus exalting, the uniform of the Poor Brothers.

Within the chapel there is a feeling of sumptuous-ness, arising, I afterwards realised, from the fine Jacobean carving, beautiful in its richness. The elaborate monument to the founder is by Nicholas Stone, master-mason to James I. One feels that the sculptor's hand must have lingered lovingly over the carving, so satisfying is the modelling of those cherubs' heads and the heraldic decorations and other embellishments. Stone has used two kinds of marble in the monument, and with them its woodwork blends most happily. But it is a pity that the tinted iron railings surrounding it, though interesting in themselves, are not in keeping, being of an earlier period.

In the right-hand corner of the chapel some of the panelling, which is from the sixteenth and seventeenth centuries, has been removed to reveal the piscina of the monks' original foundation. The effect of the grim old stones peeping out behind all that polished wood conveys an impression of irony—a defiant satirical smile, as it were—on an ancient face, challenging the durability of its modern mask.

Near by is the altar, and over it is a copy of a "Descent from the Cross," by Francis, of which the original is in the National Gallery. Besides the founder's, the chapel holds two other memorials which I was not allowed to overlook. One perpetuates the name of Dr Thomas Walker, the headmaster in the days of Steele and Addison, and the other that of Dr Matthew Raine, who was Principal in Colonel Newcome's time.

A quaint custom still prevails at the Hospital. The curfew is rung every night at eight or nine o'clock according to the time of year, the number of strokes corresponding with the number of brothers in residence.

Before leaving the ground floor, we visited a fine long chamber called after a master of the school, Brooke Hall. Brooke flourished under Cromwell's Protectorate, but was a strong Royalist, and rather a martinet at that—reasons enough for his dismissal. He appealed against this, and it seems that he was tactfully silenced with a pension and given the rooms now known by his name. Later these were converted into the dining-hall for the junior masters of the school. Brooke's portrait, full of character, hangs over the mantelpiece, whence no doubt it has been a silent observer of many convivial meals.

I was next taken through a fine old vestibule whence a marvellous Tudor staircase leads to the floor above. The staircase is adorned with delicate carvings in the best style of the period. This part of the building was annexed by Henry VIII after the suppression of the monastery in 1545. For about ten years the autocratic monarch used the place as a storehouse for his fishing-nets and tackle, as well as his hunting-gear and pavilions.

I climbed the charming staircase very slowly in order to lengthen my enjoyment of its beautiful carvings. They invite a more thorough scrutiny than I, alas, was able to make. Their rare precision —a sort of personal intimacy, as it were, between the artificer and his subject—reminded me of the wonderful reliefs adorning that exquisite home of chiselled Renaissance beauties—Blois Castle. In both examples one feels the profound devotion of the sculptor to his work.

From the landing above a door opens on to a wide terrace walk, constructed by the Duke of Norfolk, and in his time called the ambulacrum. The view

of the grassy quadrangle stretching below gives a
feeling of air and freedom, for which, in the heart of
crowded London, the lucky Carthusians should be
more than grateful. Beyond, connected by a cloistered way, were formerly the cells, or cottages, of
the monks. These cells owe their foundation to Sir
Robert Knolles, a rugged and warlike figure, spoken
of by Froissart. Each man was given a little cottage
standing in its own plot of garden. The spacious
green expanse bearing in past times a picturesquely
suggestive name—the Priory Garth—now divides
the grey old Hospital from the modern red-brick
Merchant Taylors' School.

Just at hand is a lofty room, the Officers' or
Governors' Library, where above the chimney-piece
hangs the genial portrait of Mr Daniel Wray. On
his death in 1783 his abundant collection of books
was presented to the Hospital by his widow. In
the centre of this room stands a fine mahogany
table with an admirably embossed border. All round
are set priceless ladder-backed Chippendale chairs.
These, with the table, seem to recall some grand
banquet such as we have been made familiar with
in the delightful canvases of Sir William Orchardson.
One wonders, however, to what use the furniture was
put among all those mighty tomes. They seem to
suggest a feast of reason and a flow of soul rather than
pasties, sweet dishes, and sparkling wines.

Beyond the Library is the Tapestry Room or
Great Chamber, as it was called—a splendidly pro-

portioned apartment which was part of the ducal
mansion.   Let into the ceiling recur the coat-of-arms
and motto of the Norfolk family, " Sola virtus
invicta."   The walls are hung with harmonious
Flemish tapestries.

Over the open hearth the mantelpiece is embellished with some beautiful Italian ornamental painting, thought to have been placed there about three
hundred years ago.   The rich dull-gold background
shows up the mellow tints of the pigments.   It reminded me of happy days spent in Venice, where I
had seen similar beautiful work in many of the
palaces.

From the Tapestry Chamber we went down into
the Great Hall, which formed part of the early
monastery.   It is considered by many to be the
outstanding feature of interest in the whole building,
and is a magnificent room with two galleries, added
in the sixteenth century.   One of them, by the way,
with sliding panels, was for the musicians.   Over the
ample hearth, carved in wood, are Sutton's arms.
The greyhound seen in these appears repeatedly in
Charterhouse, and had by now become to me quite
a familiar friend.

Here in this grand spacious hall the brothers
gather every day at two o'clock for their mid-
day meal.

From the hall several courtyards and ancient
passages with little old stone arches lead to the
Manciple's room, the former name for the bursar or

steward—the " Maunciple," in fact, of Chaucer's day. One of these courtyards is called the Washhouse Court, and dates back to the time when the monastery was established. These dwellings which form its quadrangle are modest and low-pitched—the mere humble relatives, as it were, of the grander domains that surround them. Nothing in all Charterhouse conveys a greater sense of age. The very cobble-stones with which the small court is paved seem embedded in antiquity.

The brothers here have indeed a sheltered life. Whatever may have been the vicissitudes of their earlier days, in Charterhouse at least they are surrounded by beautiful things, and have the leisure to contemplate them. One feels sure that their old hearts must often be filled with thankfulness for this priceless boon. What a peaceful closing to their lives was conferred upon them by Sir Thomas Sutton and his successors !

Going out into the hurly-burly of London from the quiet precincts of the Hospital, I thought what a joy it would be if one could provide a similar harbour of refuge to some of the harassed men and women of to-day.

. . . .

With Charterhouse ended my pilgrimage. Though limited, it will have achieved its aim should my readers be inspired to extend the quest for themselves.

INDEX

254

INDEX

PRINTED IN GREAT BRITAIN BY NEILL AND CO., LTD., EDINBURGH.